Jack McAfghan
Reflections on Life with My Master

A Dog's Memoir on Life After Death

Kate McGahan

I dedicate this book to my heavenly Master without whom this life would not be possible and to my earthly master without whom this book would not be possible.

"But ask the animals, now,
And let them teach you.
And the birds of the heavens,
And they shall tell you."
Job 12:7

Introduction

Love is the greatest force in the universe. It matters not if a creature has four legs or two; love applies to all of us. We all learn the most from those who love us and from those we love who don't love us in return. We learn that all the training in the world cannot touch
what love can teach.

One of our friends called me 'Einstein' because he thought I was so intelligent. Somewhere Einstein was quoted as saying that man uses only about eight percent of his brain. I've learned that there is a big difference between intelligence and wisdom. I don't know how intelligent I am per se, but I have gained wisdom from the experience of living and loving on the earth.

In the world beyond the world you think is everything is a place where it makes no matter the size of a brain or its usage. In that world there are no brains, there are only great minds filled with wisdom and hearts full of love.

Everything in this book is true. A few names and locations have been changed to respect those who wish to remain private. What you are about to read is my personal experience. It may not be true for everyone. What I have come to learn is this: Whatever we believe to be true
is what is true.
I love my truth and I have loved living it.

If I could have only one wish granted or one prayer answered it would be to always be in the right place at the right time.

Life conspires to bring lost souls together. It sets us on a course where we will intersect, sooner or later, at an appointed time and place. One step to the left or one step to the right, a moment sooner or a moment later, things might have been very different for me.

Everything is in Divine Order. Life cannot be forced. Trying to make something happen that isn't supposed to happen only brings unnecessary pain and frustration. When you trust your master, he will direct your path. You just need to trust him. All you have to do is put one foot in front of the other and follow.

At any given time, each one of us is but a moment away from the unveiling of our destiny. Until then, we have no way of knowing our life's blueprint. Some experts say that we decide the course our lives will take and the lessons we need to learn, long before we come to this planet. If that is indeed true, the knowing of it begins to leave us the moment we are born.

She had done all her research. She knew she shouldn't visit a puppy mill, but that Saturday morning she called the puppy mill lady. She wanted to see my three brothers, my sister and me. Four of our sisters had already found homes. One sister never had a chance. She was stillborn. Apparently no soul was ready when her tiny body was waiting to be filled with life. There were five of us left, waiting for our forever homes.

She drove several hours to the city and spent the day looking at dogs around town. By evening she had not found one that she couldn't walk away from. The puppy mill lady had not called her back so she called again to let them know that she would be leaving the city at 6:30 p.m. She went into a store to do some shopping and returned to her car at 6:25 p.m. She was right on schedule.

"Well," she said to herself as she started the car, "I guess I won't be finding my dog today."

As she merged onto the highway the phone rang. It was the puppy mill lady. It was 6:29 p.m.

"Hi! We're home! We'll be here all evening. The dogs are here. Come on over!"

Twenty minutes later she walked through the gate. It was a moment I'll never forget. The night was cool, the stars were bright and fragrant traces of the family dinner were lingering on the barbecue. It was the kind of moment that was so clear and vivid that I would come to remember it forever like it was yesterday. Looking back we know what moments in life are meant to be. This was one of them for me.

In a puppy mill there are dogs of all shapes, sizes, ages, breeds, and mixes. It's not the best place for a puppy to come into the world. A young couple had just come and bought two grey schnauzer-doodles. There were more dogs behind the big wooden fence whimpering, whining and barking. I never knew who was back there or why they were behind the fence.

Me, I was a mix of several breeds. At ten weeks of age, I was the ugly duckling. My sisters were born with beautiful black widow's peaks on their foreheads and the same smooth shiny coats that all my brothers had. I was blonde and scruffy. My hair was coming in thin and rough and my tail was like the tail of a weasel. I was clumsy and uncoordinated, often tripping over my own feet.

They told her that our father was a Standard Poodle and our mother was a Bearded Collie but they never mentioned my maternal grandparents who were Afghan Hounds. The puppy mill lady told her that we were "hypo allergenic", "low shed" and that we would probably weigh about 45 pounds as adults. None of it was true.

To this day I am not sure that we were all from the same family. I don't know why I was so different from the rest of them, but I was.

She thought she knew what she wanted. She specifically came to see my little sister, but by the time she arrived my sister had been sold.

"Oh..." she said as her face fell, obviously disappointed.

My brothers hovered around her, climbing all over her and into her lap. One of them was so excited he scratched her face. I just watched them all, thinking how nice it would be to be with someone like her. I hung out in the background hoping she would notice me. The others were all quite unruly, competing for her attention. I think this is where I first learned that climbing all over someone doesn't necessarily make them want to be with you.

It looked like she was going to take my little brother home. I was preparing myself for that. She was sitting on the ground and he was sitting in her lap, sleeping like a baby. Then she looked over at me for the first time and our eyes met. I could almost feel her heart touch mine. They say you fall in love in less than a second. I can verify that this is totally and utterly true.

I was overwhelmed with my feelings for her, but something in my heart told me to remain calm. I retreated to my dingy little cardboard bed, turned around a few times and lay down. I rested my head on my front paws as a humble gesture and continued to steadily gaze at her. Waiting. Watching. Hoping. I tried to crawl into her mind with my thoughts so that she would want to take me home instead of my brother. I imagined the fun the two of us would have. I pictured us playing together, walking together and discovering life together. I found myself promising God that I would be a very good dog if only He would let her notice me and make her want to take me home. As she looked across the yard at me I gently wagged my tail.

She then asked them about me.

"Oh," they said, "I don't think you want that one. He plays rough with the others. He almost killed one of the younger ones."

I felt bad when they said that but she didn't seem bothered by it. She didn't seem bothered at all.

"I kind of like him anyway, but..." she continued, "They say sometimes a dog picks you rather than you picking the dog." She gestured toward my brother in her lap and said, "Maybe this one is picking me. Maybe I'm supposed to take him?"

Oh no, I said to her, *you aren't supposed to take him. You're supposed to take me.*

All the while she was looking over at me instead of at the one in her lap. It made me feel special, the way she looked at me.

The puppy mill lady went over to her, took my brother from out of her lap, and they continued talking. I couldn't understand what they were saying, but she kept looking over at me.

"Well, guess what?" the puppy mill lady finally said, "It's official. All this guy wants is a warm lap. I don't think he is choosing you at all."

My heart did flip-flops! I lifted my head and looked at her in anticipation. Sure enough, she came right over to me and sat down at the edge of my cardboard bed.

"May I sit with you?" she asked.

Oh yes! I said, wagging my tail in welcome.

"I think this is the one," she announced with surety.

Oh I was so happy! I couldn't wait to go home with her! I didn't really like this place that was my first home.

Then she took me completely by surprise. She went and left me there! She talked a little more to the puppy mill lady and the next thing I knew, she was leaving! She kept looking at me with a sweet look of longing even as she walked back through the gate and closed the latch. I put my head down again, accepting the fact that I might not have a forever home.

I dreamed of her many times in the days that followed.

She returned home and, even though she liked me a lot, she wasn't sure she could make the commitment to a ten-week old puppy. Two weeks later she cast her fear aside and called the puppy mill lady.

"Do you still have that little blonde one?"

"Oh, yes. He's still here. He's been waiting for you."

Oh how I had been waiting! My brothers were all gone. A lot of the others were gone too. I didn't know where she went! I thought she was gone forever! I was beginning to think that nobody wanted me, but she did. She wanted me after all.

This time she came through the gate and she saw me right away. She had a big smile on her face and she only had eyes for me. The puppy mill lady greeted her with a handshake.

"Welcome back, Kate."

She. Kate. I liked her name. It had a familiar ring to it.

"It's a big decision for me," Kate said to the lady, "but I think I'm doing the right thing."

"Of course you are. Come with me." The lady didn't seem too interested in any of the reasons for anything.

I followed them as far as the screen door of the house and waited for her there.

"That will be $250," said the puppy mill lady. "If he dies in the first six months you get a $250 credit towards any dog you want."

"He'd better not die because he's the dog I want," said Kate as she wrote the check. She glanced over at me furtively through the screen door like she couldn't get me out of there fast enough.

I rode home in her lap. It was my first ride in a car, watching trees and clouds and rooftops go by. Kate seemed to enjoy watching me watch the world come into being. I looked forward with pure anticipation. I could feel the joy in her heart and somehow I knew it was because of me and joy grew in my heart too.

Love can be found in unexpected places. Sometimes we go out searching for what we think we want and we end up with what we're supposed to have. Kate originally wanted a low shed poodle mix. When she chose me she thought she was getting a medium sized collie-poo. What she actually got was a large mixed breed Afghan Hound. She thought she knew what she wanted but God knew what she needed. He knew what I needed too, for the moment that she became my master was the moment I truly began to live.

She thought she chose me but I chose her. I wanted her so much that I had imagined her wanting me as much as I wanted her. I believed that if I concentrated hard enough that it would come to be. I imagined living with her. I dreamed of her from the moment she walked out that gate until she came back for me. This is when I started learning the power of the mind. It always works as long as you don't get desperate or impatient and as long as you keep your heart in the right place and your master at the forefront.

"Welcome home," she said to me as we walked across the threshold of the big front door. "This is where you live now. Our home is your home, Jack, always and forever."

Not all dogs are perfect dogs, but all dogs are inherently good. Like people, we are affected by environment and circumstance. Some breeds get a bad rap because sometimes humans breed them to be a certain way, like overly macho or protective. In our life on earth we are dependent on humans for everything, including our breeding. We can be bred for aggression or we can be bred for peace.

Sometimes things go wrong. I heard one of my brothers was returned to the puppy mill. A blonde lady had bought him. I remember her. She wore pretty clothes and high heels and smelled of expensive perfume. She made an excitable fuss over him that day. I was relieved that she didn't pick me. I was reeling from her perfume and there was something about her that made me nervous. She brought with her a little plastic bag of raw ground beef that she fed the puppies when the puppy mill lady wasn't looking. I didn't take part in any of it but I watched my brother eat and eat and eat. I guess the lady just picked the one who could eat the most.

The first thing he did 'wrong' was to throw up in her fancy car on their way home. She blamed him for that, which is too bad because I'm sure it was the meat that she fed him that made him sick. None of us had ever eaten anything but kibble. On top of that he had never ridden in a car before so he no doubt had motion sickness too. She probably never even thought to open the car window to give him air.

At home she didn't have much time for him. She worked all day, leaving him alone to freely chew on things around the house. He also had puppy accidents on her oriental rugs and hardwood floors. A few months later she took him back to the puppy mill lady.

"I want another dog," she demanded, "this one is the dog from hell!"

She was wrong. It said more about her than it did about my brother. No dogs come from hell. We come from the same place people do. We all come from Heaven. We're all from the right place; it's just that some of us get into the wrong hands.

Kate had an older dog at home as well. They had been together for many years and life for them had become quiet and predictable. I didn't understand that their world was turned upside down because of me. I had so much to learn! Kate worked long and hard to train me in the ways of living in a house with a family and good manners.

Their life changed considerably. They weren't used to having a goofball like me around. When I would try to amuse and entertain, Kate would raise her eyebrows, look over at Grady and say, "Oh my old girl, what have we done?" She would gaze back at me, dazed and dazzled, while I ran and jumped around like a kangaroo all over the house. I couldn't help it, I was so happy to be living with her!

She was learning too and she started having more fun in her life. She would laugh with me and call me names like "JackaROO!" and "Jack in the Box". She sang songs to me like 'Jumping Jack Flash' and 'Ooo-Ooo-Ooo-Oooo Jackie Blue'! She would sing and I would dance around like crazy; it was so much fun! Sometimes she would even dance too. I loved everything but most of all I loved to see her happy.

On the other hand she was very sensitive. Sometimes she would sit quietly with me in the evening and hold me close. I really liked the quiet times because we had worked very hard during the day and I was always ready to be calm and relaxed at the end of it. She would softly sing me lullabies and love songs that she said were written just for us. I knew those songs. They were love songs that God wrote for us through someone who could write them, so that we could sing them back to Him and to each other. Just listen the next time you hear your favorite love song and you will realize it was meant for you to sing to Him and for Him to sing to you.

That night I wrote my first love song, for my master on earth, for my Master in Heaven and for lovers everywhere.

Oh My Friend,
The moment I looked in your eyes,
I saw your soul and you saw mine.
You saved me from the life I knew.
I dreamed that everything was you.
You brought me home and there I learned
This life was made for you and me.
~~~~~~~~~~~~

Sometimes when she sat with me she would feel the beating of my heart. It would beat slowly and then quickly and then slowly again. Sometimes it beat so fast that she couldn't count the beats because they all ran together. She had never had a puppy mill dog but she had heard horror stories about dogs that were sick because of bad breeding.

Each night we would sit quietly on the bedroom floor after Grady was fast asleep. Kate would look into my eyes.

"It's time for our prayers," she would say. She would put the hollows of her hands on my chest and hold me close, imagining my heart beating in time with hers and in time with the ticking of the clock by the bed.

Our prayers must have been answered because over time our hearts were beating exactly the same.

She was a very rational person until the moment I would start to pee on the floor. She would drop whatever it was she was doing and scream.

"No, Jack, no! You pee outside!"

It startled me to no end when she would snatch me up, racing for the door to usher me out. Over and over she did this when I would pee in the house.

At one point she put some pretty bells on the door and every time we'd reach the door she would jingle them. It made it kind of fun like a game! It was not too long after that that I learned to jingle the bells when it was time to go out. Oh, it made her so happy! She would smile and say, "Good Boy, Jack!" She was so happy when I jingled the bells that I learned to jingle them just to see her happy. After awhile she would rush to the door only to smirk at me and say "You silly boy! You're supposed to jingle the bells when you need to go out, not when you just want attention."

She was right. I just wanted her attention. I just wanted her.

Some days we would get up and have breakfast at the crack of dawn, sometimes much later. Us dogs never planned on anything because every day was different with her. We never asked for anything. We never knew when the day would start, when it would end or what would happen in between. We learned not to expect anything and we just put all our faith in our master. We were very happy and we always knew that our needs would be met, sooner or later.

Many days Kate would go into the office. She'd leave early in the morning and on good days she'd come home for lunch. When she did she would steal glances at the clock the whole time, cherishing each and every moment with us. I didn't understand why she spent so much time looking at the clock because it just took away from our time together. All too soon she'd rush back to work, saying, "I've got to go but I'll be back!" She would call out "I Love You!" from the car as she drove up the road. We would run from window to window until we couldn't see or hear her anymore.

Late in the day she'd return home. We'd all eat dinner together and then go for a walk. It seemed that her work was never done. She would often be on her computer until the wee hours of the morning. Her bed was always covered with books and pens and papers but she always managed to make room for Grady and me.

Each night she would get into bed with a big sigh of relief that she had survived another day. "Ahh," she would say, settling back into her pillows, "here's the best part of my day." It was the best part of our day too.

I would rest my chin on the edge of the bed and look at her with pleading eyes. It was a game that I always would win.

"Hey there Jack, do you want to come up on the bed?" she would ask me each time.

"OK," she'd answer for me, "but stay on the blanket! C'mon!" She would pat the bed briskly and say "Yay!" as I jumped up. I would get into just the right comfy position on the lower half of the bed...and always on the blanket. I would face the bedroom door to protect her but I kept an eye on her too.

When I was little she would let me sleep wherever I wanted, but when I got bigger I hogged most of the bed. I didn't mean to, I just didn't know how big I was. I'd lie there like I was a person too, with my head on the pillow next to hers.

By the time I grew to full size, we had the bed to ourselves. Grady had become too frail to jump up on it, but she didn't really seem to care because at that point she would pretty much fall asleep wherever she was. As time went on it seemed that Grady was sleeping more and more

I loved it when she read out loud to me. We read lots of books. She would always get excited when she read something she had never thought about before. If it excited her, it excited me too. We learned together many things we never knew.

I distinctly remember one night when she was reading a book called "How To Get Someone To Fall In Love With You." I looked at her in disbelief, for I loved her as much anyone could love anyone. She didn't need to be reading those books. She already knew everything she needed to know.

You didn't need to do anything for me to fall in love with you.

She glanced up at me when I said that to her.

"I know you know that I love you," she said, "and I know that you love me too".

I would hear about her day as we fell asleep. I would hear about her dreams when we woke up. She kept a notebook on the table by her bed where she would write down her dreams and her interpretations of them. Some of them were quite entertaining with twisted plots and storylines. As for me, I would usually just dream about eating, running and hunting. My favorite dream was of a pretty cream-colored girl. She was with me in a peaceful Afghanistan paradise. We would run together for hundreds of miles, leaping over the rolling rivers and prancing through the rugged mountains. My love and I, we are full of joy and we run like the wind!

One morning Kate wrote in her notebook about "The Hawk Dream". She told me about it and it was amazing for I, too, had dreamed the very same dream that night. A giant hawk swooped down and picked me up, its talons gripping my back, and it carried me high across the sky. It was a wonderful dream for me but for some reason she was really disturbed by it. She thought it was a premonition that perhaps one day I would be abducted by a predator. I told her not to worry because the dream with Hawk was just an exciting ride. I joked with her about how I get "carried away" sometimes. I laughed and she laughed, but she always worried about what The Hawk Dream really meant.

Sometimes Kate would go away on business trips. She always got us the best dog sitters but even so I would miss her a lot even though I was pretty cool about it.

Meanwhile, Grady was a big worrywart. She couldn't seem to quiet her heart. She was very restless most of the time and she couldn't sit still. When Kate left the house she would get crazy-desperate and rip up drapes and claw through window screens and mini blinds. She would destroy whatever was blocking the doors or the windows in her hopes of breaking out of the house. Her mission: To Find Kate. There was nothing I could do but stand there and watch her tear things apart. Once she got outside she would wander around helplessly, not really knowing where to go once she got there.

Our master would never abandon us, I would tell her. *When you worry it only makes matters worse.* I tried to reassure her but she didn't respect me because I was still a puppy and she was all grown up so what did I know?

As Grady got older her anxiety increased. I thought it might be my fault but Kate said no, it wasn't my fault at all. It was just Grady getting older. The vet gave Grady a prescription for doggie Valium. Kate had the prescription filled but then decided against it after reading the potential side effects.

One day, many replaced screens and window blinds later, Grady had been exceptionally destructive. Kate pointed her finger at her and said sternly, "If you continue this behavior you will have to stay in the garage. You cannot keep doing this!"

It's really important to talk to your pet and let them know what is expected, especially when you've had the last straw. Grady got a little better; just enough for Kate to see that she was making an effort. I don't think Kate ever would have sent Grady to the garage. She was just playing the kind of game we all play to get someone to do something.

The bottom line was that Grady had been abused and abandoned before she ever found Kate. She was more set in her ways than most dogs and for a dog like Grady it was very difficult to unlearn what she had learned the hard way. Abandonment had grown into her character. Kate tried to relieve her but she carried the fear of it with her for the rest of her life.

There was a time Kate dated a guy who drank too much. His hands would shake as he held his glass. She thought he drank because he didn't feel loved. She thought she could love him out of his drinking but what she didn't realize was that he didn't start drinking because of her and he wasn't going to stop because of her. In the same way, something had happened to Grady long before we came along and, no matter how hard we tried, we could not undo all the damage that had been done. We could only live in such a way as to minimize the triggers that created her discomfort.

I was glad I didn't have the anxiety that Grady had. I always felt that whenever Kate left, wherever she went, it was like we were still together. No matter how many miles came between us, I could always feel her. It was like we were still connected. If she was happy, sad or stressed, I could feel it across the miles. I could tell when she was on her way home. When she got off the plane and into her car two hours away, I could feel her say, "I'm almost home Jack and Grady! I'll be back real soon!" It would be a little while and we would all be together again.

I had faith in her. I knew my master would always come back. I knew my master would never abandon me.

Life became more stressful. We were seeing less and less of Kate. She was working all the time it seemed. One day we were sick, all three of us. I think Kate was getting sick because of the stress of her job. This particular day she was cleaning up our messes and was getting sick doing it. She laughed cynically, "It can't get any worse than this!" After a couple of days she took us to the vet who gave us pills to treat our diarrhea.

When we came home from the vet we had a pill with our dinner. We had a pill with our breakfast the next morning. Oh, we were already feeling so much better! Kate was still sick but she was relieved that the medicine was effective for us. I was jumping around again and Grady was feeling pretty good too.

Later that day Kate was in her car on the way home from work and, as she came to a stop at the stoplight, a red plastic medicine bottle rolled out from under her front seat. It was the medicine for our diarrhea. It had never been opened. She was confused. What had she been giving us?

The first thing she did upon arriving home was to go to the cupboard where there was an identical red plastic medicine bottle with pills in it. It's what she had given us with dinner and breakfast. She looked at the label. It was Grady's doggie Valium. She had given us both two doses of Valium for our diarrhea. The funny thing is that it actually cured it.

Her stress was actually making us sick too. We are very sensitive to our humans. We are tethered to each other in invisible ways.

Grady taught me a lot. She taught me how to stay on the porch while Kate was out working in the yard. She tried to model for me how to walk on the leash. I used to watch her with admiration, but when the leash was actually attached to my neck it was very uncomfortable. I thought I would choke! Like a bucking bronco at the end of a rope, I just wanted to be free of it! Eventually I made peace with the leash. I learned that things just get worse when you struggle with something you cannot change. The day came when I would find myself getting excited when Kate would get the leash out because I knew it meant we were going for a walk; another adventure through the world.

I used to have a blast playing with Grady. She was a really good sport. Every so often, I would knock her over after running across the yard towards her at full speed. I was like a bull going after a matador in the ring. I was too young to understand that she was getting frail. Sometimes in my blind eagerness to see Kate, I would brush past Grady who would inevitably end up falling into the rose bushes or back down the stairs or some such thing. Nonetheless, Grady always forgave me.

Grady was very much a homebody. Girls seem to stay closer to home than boys. She was always waiting on the porch for me whenever I came back to the house. Even when she was weak with arthritis, she would hoist herself up as soon as I approached. She would stand at the top of the stairs barking her head off with her tail wagging to and fro, as if she were the one in charge.

I was younger and stronger than she, it was clear. I liked to think I was smarter too. Once in awhile Kate would give us little bacon-wrapped rawhide bones. Grady would get totally absorbed in hers. While she was gnawing and chomping, I would take mine and hide it. As soon as she was done with hers I'd go get mine. I loved to drive her crazy. I would stand right in her face and chew it dramatically, making lots of noise with it as it tastily rattled around in my teeth. I knew she would smell it and hear it and see it and then she would want it too! It was a good activity to liven up our day.

I would then drop the bone, as if by accident, right beside her. *Uh oh!* Her lips would immediately curl back into a threatening growl and I would start whining. *Oh no!* It was just a game we played. It would go on for quite some time, mostly because I never knew when to quit. I would try to retrieve my rawhide bone and she would growl and show her teeth to intimidate me. She would always win and I would find out that I was not so smart after all. The rawhide game was the only game Grady could win but actually I won too because I knew she needed to win at something and it was always a really fun game to play.

Kate was spending more and more time with Grady. She often said the same things to Grady that she had said to me when I was a puppy. Grady would pee on the rug and as she did Kate would drop whatever she was doing and run over to her, "No Grady, No! Not on the rug!" but Grady couldn't help it.

A dog relies on its senses to understand things. Once in awhile I would try to imagine what life was like for Grady when she could no longer see and no longer hear. I didn't think about it for too long. I hoped that I would never get that old. Grady eventually became blind, deaf and she couldn't hold her bladder but she still had a sense of humor and her tail still wagged. Kate would say, "As long as her tail is wagging, we'll keep her going."

A dog can wag its tail but a dog needs more than that. Just like a person needs a purpose, a dog needs a purpose too. We don't feel good when we are just taking up space. Grady had been a successful therapy dog many years before. We all need to be successful at something for as long as we live.

One of our friends was a veteran rescue dog from the World Trade Center. He had many stories about rescuing people from the wreckage. We learned a lot from him. He told us that when the buildings went down many rescue workers arrived on site, including specially trained dogs from all over the country. He was one of them. The mission of the dogs was to find survivors and victims. All too soon the unfortunate time came when no more could be found. At this point many of the dogs became listless and depressed. They refused to eat or drink. They failed to thrive. They did not feel the desire to live because they were simply not able to fulfill their purpose.

Being able to do something we're good at prolongs our life and promotes our sense of well-being. If we don't have a job to do, a task to accomplish, or someone to serve on a regular basis we will create our own opportunities. We will chase lizards and rabbits, obsess about squirrels and other mammals, bark at everyone who passes by or rearrange the rugs in the house. We can always find something to do if our humans don't need us or provide us with work to do.

Time never existed for me but I could always feel its passage. I was sensitive to the comings and goings of life. The clock would tick on the kitchen wall. She would turn the calendar pages. Everything has a season it is true.

I could sense "time" only by how my world felt to me. Days and nights were easy to define. It was light; it was dark. The days would shorten, lengthen and shorten again. It was hot, it was cold; leaves would fall; seasons would change. Things would die and be reborn. Perennials would thrive, decline and then, once again burst forth with life when the warmth of the sun returned. It was one thing we knew we could depend on: the cycle of change and renewal.

Every year I was quite jealous of a certain little bird that visited in early spring until summer. Kate was always happy when it returned because it meant that the warmer weather was coming. It had a breathy high-pitched whistle. "Ssssssesesesese!" She would imitate it and they would talk back and forth to each other. I'd come running from wherever I was and demand of her: *Where is he? What are you doing talking to him again?* I would yap and whine and jump around. She would just laugh and tell me I was silly to worry; that she loved me best.

"You're the best boy in the world," she would say.

The only thing we could count on was that everything would change. Something is always turning into something else. There was only one constant as the days passed. All of the time and all year round I could feel her love for us in the air, wafting like incense over the uneven terrain of our life.

Every year the weed season kept us very busy. My long hair seemed to grab every seed that needed a ride. Kate would spend many hours brushing and combing and picking every clinging thorn out of my hair. Some of them would be embedded in my skin and they hurt a lot but I never uttered a sound. I knew it would pass. I knew she would take care of me. She always did.

One evening, at the end of the summer, we walked to the National Forest. Grady didn't want to go, she just wanted to sleep, so the two of us set out on a soft path through a beautiful part of the forest trail. At one point on our hike we got very playful. It was the energy of the place. It just felt really good to be there together.

At the curve in the trail we were both running as fast as we could go! We were having so much fun! Suddenly we screeched to a halt for we found ourselves in the middle of a field of goatheads, burdocks and other spiny thorns. We had been having so much fun that we didn't feel ourselves getting covered with them! We were trapped! The only way out was to go back through them. I refused to move. Meanwhile it was getting dark and the coyotes were beginning to howl. I didn't care. I wasn't moving.

She had stickers all over her sneakers and the bottoms of her pants and I had them all over me! They were embedded in the pads of my paws and my tail and in my long hair too. My paws were like pincushions! It was too painful to take a single step and I knew each one would only lead me further, deeper and deeper, into the weeds.

She was getting nervous because night was falling. I was nervous only because she was nervous. I just stood there. I trusted her to figure it out.

She picked each and every goat head off of the pads of my feet. Still I wouldn't budge. Then she had an idea. Moving backwards she, with me in front of her, cleared a trail and guided me all the way back the way we had come. I was hesitant at first but eventually, one step at a time I found that each footfall was clear. Like a good guide dog she cleared a safe and open path for me

Finally we were out! We walked home where we spent several hours pulling the remaining stickers off of her and off of me. It was a difficult experience and yet when you can put your trust in the one you're with, you come out of it all right. It is times like this that permanently weave the one you love into the fabric of your being.

Leaves started to fall, composting into the moist autumn earth. There was a chill in the air. I no longer could detect the smells of the forest trail on the southern breeze. I sensed changes coming and it made me uneasy.

After many seasons of carrying Grady around and cleaning up after her, the day came when Kate sat down to talk with her. She put her hands on Grady's chest like she had done with me when I was little. With her hands cupped over Grady's heart, she told her how much she appreciated the years they had shared together. She told her how much she loved her. While she talked with her, she gently combed her sheltie fur and cleaned her eyes. She had to clean her eyes all the time because they would get gunk in them. Grady hadn't been able to tolerate going to grooming salon for a very long time. Even at her best she never cared to be fussed over or petted too much for too long although now she seemed more relaxed and less resistant. Sometimes it feels really good to finally surrender to someone you love and trust. It takes some of us all of our lives to arrive at this point.

I was a little jealous that Grady was getting so much attention but I knew that something important was taking place, I didn't quite know what. I was still a puppy and too young to understand.

Kate was a good master. She carried Grady when she couldn't walk and she protected her from things that would upset and exhaust her. She made sure Grady knew that she was not alone.

Grady wasn't going upstairs anymore. She had a bed on the floor near the fireplace downstairs. Kate and I had been sleeping on the couch down there for quite some time. This particular night Kate slept on the floor beside Grady until morning.

In the morning Grady and I went outside. It was exceptionally warm and sunny and it was the first good day Grady had had in a long time! We came in and ate our breakfast and shared some together time. Then Kate carried Grady to the car and I followed. I was surprised to see that Kate had set up our car like a cozy little den. Grady's favorite quilt covered the backseat and there were pillows all around. Grady's favorite toys were in there too. It was kind of fun to have it that way.

But it wasn't much fun this particular day. Grady would typically sit in the back where she could see Kate and where Kate could see her but this time Grady positioned herself right behind the driver's seat where they couldn't see each other at all. I knew Grady didn't want Kate to see her but I didn't know why. I sat on the other side where I could see Kate, who was crying silently. For some reason she didn't want Grady to know that she was crying. She didn't want Grady to see her either. I felt an overwhelming sadness in our car.

A little while later we pulled into the parking lot at the veterinary clinic. Grady always hated the vet. Me, I loved going because of all the pretty girls in there who loved me and who always made a big fuss over me.

"Hi Handsome!" They would always greet me smiling and laughing. It was like a big fun reunion party every time we went! When she took me in to meet them for the very first time they asked her, "Why? Why did you get another dog?"

"I just felt like I needed a backup plan," was her reply.

A backup plan? I'm a backup plan?

She told them she got me in case she lost Grady. She apparently didn't think she could live alone without Grady by her side. She had learned to love her very much and was very attached to her. Sometimes when you love like that you forget that you are strong enough to make it on your own.

I never knew this. Wow, I am just a backup plan...?

Then she looked over at me proudly and said, "Can you blame me? Who could resist him if they saw him? Why, anyone would want to take him home! I'm so lucky it was me!"

Cool. And I was lucky too.

This time at the clinic was not like the other times. This time we never got out of the car. Kate joined us in the back seat, resting one hand on Grady and the other hand on me.

"Everything's okay," she reassured us.

The vet came out to the car with her assistant. They put a couple of needles into Grady's leg. It got strangely quiet and in just a few moments the vet said, "She's gone".

Kate said "Thank you," smiling weakly as they were leaving. I watched her. I watched Grady. I didn't fully understand but I knew that something amazing, maybe even miraculous, had just happened. Grady was so quiet and still. It was as if a great weight had lifted and in its place was absolute peace.

Grady just lay there with her eyes closed. She had not been groomed in many months and yet she looked like a beauty queen! Her shining hair glistened in the morning sun as the breeze drifted in tossing it gently about. Her eyes were surprisingly clean and clear.

Kate had always worried that if she made the decision to put Grady to sleep that she would be "playing God." She had been waiting for God to call for Grady who suffered year after year, but God just didn't call for Grady. After awhile she got to thinking that maybe this was just a test of her love. Maybe it was a test to see if she loved Grady enough to let her go. I hope she never has to make that kind of decision for me.

We drove the car to the back of the clinic where there was a big heavy door. A nice girl named Joy came to the car and lifted Grady out. Grady looked so beautiful, draped in the arms of Joy. Joy carried her through the big door and I never saw Grady again. I finally understood. I knew that she was in a good place. I knew that she had gone Home. I don't know how I knew this but I did.

After the big door closed, Kate looked at me smiling with tears in her eyes.

"Well, Jackie, let's go home. I've got a little boy to take care of."

She was trying to smile but I knew she was sad. I was glad I was her little boy and that she wanted to take care of me. Even if it meant being a backup plan, I'm in! I knew we were going back home and this made me happy. I had the sense that Grady was happy because she was going Home too.

That was the day Kate vowed to help people come to terms with putting their dogs to sleep. After all, she had agonized for many years over it. She dwelled on it long before Grady was frail. She had been afraid of it for a very long time and she learned that ultimately there was nothing at all to be afraid of. She found that it was much easier to actually carry it out than to anticipate and fear it.

"Grady was so beautiful and at peace," she would tell them. "I should have done it a long time ago." "I know she's in a better place." She would share the story, but most people have to decide for themselves in their own way and in their own time.

Us dogs typically don't speak much English. If I didn't do something she wanted me to do or if I did something she didn't want me to do, it was usually because she didn't clearly let me know what was expected of me. She was very patient though. She'd say, "It's okay Jack. I know you're doing your best."

Meanwhile she was my master and she could do anything and everything! She could open cans. She drove a car. She could go to the store with money she made to pay for our dinner. She played the piano and planted trees and flowers. She built our house and made it our home.

She was busy almost all the time. Her 'In a minute...' became much longer and her 'I'll be back soon!' could stretch until the sun went down. I would wait a minute or an hour or more, it didn't matter. She would always do what she said she would do, eventually. I was beginning to understand her and I was glad that I never had a well-developed concept of time. It came in very handy to have it not matter.

She tried to learn about me and understand me. I was trying to understand her too. She read a lot of books about dog behavior and as we got older she realized that it was really up to her to help us to build the relationship she wanted us to have. As my master, she had the power to create me and shape me. She did this by teaching me, by correcting me and by loving me. Above all, by loving me.

I was very obedient for I loved her too and I wanted to please her. She only had to tell me something once or twice before I learned it. I kept getting bigger and bigger. I surpassed the predicted 45-pound mark; I never seemed to stop growing! As I grew my perspective kept shifting and with the shift the rules would change too.

The day came when I was tall enough for my head to clear the dining room table. Wow. I was eye to eye with her dinner plate and I could see her eating things that I would like to eat too. She would put her fork down, look at me sternly and say: "You stop that. Begging doesn't get you anywhere."

She always ate first and then fed me afterwards, like a good alpha dog does. It was usually worth waiting for because I would inevitably get a little bit of everything that had been on her plate. It's just like everything else. If you think positive and are obedient and accepting, what you want has a way of ending up on your plate.

At its best, communication can be a challenge, but there were a few things that came easily for both of us. A lightweight wag of my tail was the same as her smile; my "power wag" was her laugh. My favorite thing to do with her was to run and play and smile and wag and laugh!

We looked at each other a lot. We studied each other. That's what you do when you love someone. You want to understand them. You want to be able to see the world the way they see it. You want to know them. You don't ever want to stop looking at them and learning about them.

We would look at each other across a field, across a room, even in a mirror. Once, only once, when we were gazing at each other, I felt that I was actually her. It was mystifying. I could see myself looking back at myself from her eyes. I am not sure if I was she or she was me but I was sure in that moment that we were one and the same. I felt only love and nothing else. This was the moment I first became aware of myself and this is the only reason that I can write this book.

Even though we spoke different languages, I had a range of voices to communicate different things. I was pretty quiet most of the time. My gentle warning "woof" would alert her to something I found suspicious. She would always stop what she was doing to come to see what I was looking at.

"Shh..." she would say and with our heads close together we would quietly assess the situation. She never wanted me to feel that I needed to bark to get her attention. When you say something quietly it can be more effective than when you yell about it.

I learned from Grady that it only upsets you more to whine and bark about something. It was actually her own barking that triggered her anxiety and it became a vicious cycle. To find peace in the confusion and chaos of life, one needs to approach things from a calm position whenever possible.

Sometimes, however, I would get so excited about something that I would totally forget my manners. I was so happy when our friends came to the house that I would jump, electrified, all over them. In my joy I forgot what I learned as a pup: to leave them wanting more of me, not less.

If a stranger approached too quickly or caught me off guard, or if someone had a big hat on their head or a hood or hair piled up on top, I just couldn't help it. "Awo-OOOooo!" I just couldn't suppress my ancestral hound dog howl. When I barked like this, it would get her immediate attention. She would run to see what I was howling at and say, "Oh Jack, oh my goodness!" I couldn't really control it; it just came out when I least expected it.

She said that it was all because of me that our house and lives were safe. She thanked me every day for protecting her and our home. It made me very proud and helped me to know that I was doing a good job.

In my years with her I came to witness and respect our similarities. She too yelped, growled, barked, whined and sighed...and in those times I felt I understood her more than any other time.

In the old days I used to jump all over her when she came through the door. I couldn't contain myself! It was the best part of the day, being reunited! She would say how she missed me and would kiss me and hug me and love me, but then one day I guess she felt I was too old for that kind of thing and probably too big for it too. She signed us up for Obedience Training Class at Four Paws Academy.

At our first class, the teacher suggested we bring clickers, treats or squeaker toys to reward for jobs well done. The fact is I needed no reward but Kate's praise and her love. That's why I was doing this. I wasn't doing it for treats or toys. I was doing this for her. I was doing this for us.

She was learning a lot of important things in class too. When one of us learned, we both learned. While I was learning boundaries, she was too. We were both learning about give and take, trust, consistency and discipline. We also learned how lucky we were to have each other. We made a good team.

She never yelled that she was the boss but she was. She let me know in unique and creative ways. For example on our walks if I was heading one way on the leash, like a good master she would sometimes catch me off guard, purposefully changing direction to keep me on my toes.

"C'mon Jack, we're going this way," she would say crisply, reminding me that she's the one in charge. A gentle tug on the leash and I would adjust myself quickly. I never questioned it. I knew that she knew where we were going and I never once looked back. Sometimes God does that too. He reminds us not to get too headstrong so that we remain humble and attentive to Him. He knows where He is taking us.

Without a master to discipline us, without a master to provide rules for living, without visible and invisible fences to protect us, our lives can be chaotic at best. Like children, dogs need to know their limits. Dogs need a certain structure in life to feel safe. Most of the time when there is a dog that doesn't behave well it's because he hasn't had the proper structure provided for him. He doesn't know his boundaries or what is expected of him. It's up to his master to lay the ground rules so that he can be happy, healthy, comfortable and obedient.

One day she totally ignored me when she came through the door. It was very out of character for her. I jumped and jumped! I jumped even higher and harder to get her to respond but she just wouldn't. She even turned her back on me! I soon came to realize that we had both grown up and that jumping wasn't necessary. The rules were different now. From that point on I just stopped jumping altogether.

Training, for some, includes shock and choker collars and strict demands to obey. I noticed that we were different than the others. We didn't need these things. Instead of barking orders, she would encourage me. She treated me like a teammate. She would invite me rather than tell me. She would use her hands so I could see and hear and smell her all at the same time. Instead of "Heel," she would command, "Walk with me." Instead of "Stay," she would say, "Stay with me." Instead of "Wait," she would command, "Wait for me." She reminded me that she was always an important part of everything we did. We worked together to succeed and there was nothing we couldn't accomplish.

Many dogs get the word "wait" and the word "stay" mixed up. When she would say, "Wait," I would not move until she came back for me. When she said, "Stay," I would not move until she called for me to "Come" to her. Stay means: "Stay I'll be calling you to come". Wait means: "Wait right there until I come back for you." I notice lots of people use these two words interchangeably and it can be very confusing.

Learning the Wait command came in quite handy because I would often find myself in the position of waiting for her. I would wait and wait and wait...and wait. Once we understand your commands, once we trust that you will always do what you say you will do, we will wait forever for you. We will come whenever you call.

I especially liked Group Obedience Training. It was kind of like being back at the puppy mill or at the dog park because we made lots of friends. We would be given a homework assignment and have to work on it. In the next class we were to show everyone in the group how good we were at knowing the commands and completing the task. You could always tell which dogs loved their masters the most because they were always the most obedient and successful.

I was very glad that she was soft spoken. There was one lady at class who was always hollering at her dog. *You don't have to yell, I can hear you just fine*, the dog would respond, but the lady would yell anyway. She was so busy yelling she could never ever hear what her dog had to say.

So many people feel they have to yell at their dogs to get their attention. You don't have to yell at us at all. Just look into our eyes and speak the words you need to speak; words we might even understand, and tell us with your heart what you want from us. That's all you need to do. We'll always try to give you what we think it is you want.

She always said I did her proud. I never had to work too long to learn something. I always wanted to please her. I was so happy for her when they praised me for doing well because I know it reflected what a good master she was. I was happy for anyone in the class who was praised for doing a good job! She said I was the only dog in the class who would wag its tail when another dog accomplished something. I just wanted everyone to be happy and successful!

Most of all I wanted her to be proud of me. I worked hard because I loved her. As I matured, each task was another opportunity to show her my love and obedience. I excelled because I honored her. I wanted everyone to know what an amazing master she was to have a dog as obedient, as faithful, and as loving as me.

Life wasn't perfect after training. I had some things that worked against me as a result of my genetics. I inherited my long nose from my ancestors who were sighthounds. My nose was good for sniffing things out but it also contributed to my precision long distance eyesight. My grandfather came from a long line of esteemed hunters. Not only were they fast runners and team players; they could spot a rabbit or a fox a great distance away.

Most puppies when they are born develop their sense of smell first. My sense of sight developed first. Us sighthounds carry this strength with us forever, for better and for worse.

When I would see something I was interested in, it didn't matter how much I loved her. I would get so focused on what I was looking at that I didn't see, hear, smell, feel or think about anything else. She would be calling for me as if from the far recesses of my mind while my entire being was riveted on a rabbit across the road. She would have to stand right in front of me to block my view and divert my attention so that I would see her and hear her. A sighthound's focus is always on what it is looking at. I am glad to report however, that one of my favorite things to look at was her.

We would watch TV on Saturday nights. She was always considerate of me when she picked the programs. Lots of times we would watch documentaries about wild animals or trainers and their challenging dogs. I cannot believe what some dogs try to get away with.

It was kind of funny how sometimes her friends would come over just to watch me watch TV. They seemed to find this quite entertaining. Sometimes we would just watch YouTube. She would search for videos of "Afghan Hound – Bearded Collie - Standard Poodle". I always identified most with my Afghan Hound roots but I have to say that Zoe the Bearded Collie really captured my attention. He acted a lot like me. He's how I knew I had Bearded Collie in me for sure. We can learn a lot about ourselves when we are able to recognize ourselves in someone else.

We lived in a great neighborhood. Lots of people had dogs and they walked on the road near our house. My first friend there was Shanti. "Namaste," she would say graciously as she greeted me, which means " The God in me acknowledges the God in you." She was very evolved and wise. Sasha, Akita, Quigley and Cricket were my friends too. I would always greet them enthusiastically and I would always be sure to extend a courteous hello to their humans as well. There was a family of dachshunds I knew but I never could remember all their little names. I befriended a pug whose name I still can't spell or pronounce but we got along really well anyway.

One neighbor had a German Shepherd puppy. We played a lot and she was great fun. When she was about eight months old, a sick and vicious dog attacked her. If a dog has an incident like this early enough in life they often never get over it. We were never allowed to play again after that. She and her owner would walk straight down the road as if they had blinders on, while I would be wagging my tail at the edge of our yard to say hello...to no avail. We learn early that friends come and that friends go. We learn that all we can count on is that things will change. Fortunately dogs live in the moment so we aren't bothered for too long by most of it.

The hardest part about having a big yard was the learning to stay in it. I always wanted to go out to explore the surrounding neighborhood. Even when I thought she wasn't looking, Kate would seem to know the very moment I headed towards the road. As soon as my paw touched the asphalt, she would come out of seeming nowhere and speak sharply, "No Jack, no. You stay in your yard!"

She would command me to stay in our yard but then her friends would meet up while walking their dogs. They would stand and talk to each other just a few feet away from me, right in the middle of the road. They would see me there and call my name and I would happily run out into the road to greet them. I would get in big trouble for it! I didn't understand. Why are they in the road if we aren't supposed to go into the road? Looking back, they were silly to stand in the middle of the road and talk. It was funny how they would scatter like flies when a car or truck came driving by and then they would simply gather again, right back in the middle of the road.

Kate was determined to teach me to avoid the road. We had an annoying exercise that we did several times a day. We would walk, me on my leash and her at the helm, along the edges of our property, over and over again. It was very tedious.

She was trying to teach me the boundary lines but I didn't like boundaries. Nobody does at first. She would throw her hands up in frustration until one day she got smart about it. She would stand in the road, making me wait at the edge of our yard on the leash and she would entice me to "Come!" to her into the road where she was standing. It was a bit confusing but of course I would go. As soon as my paw hit the pavement she would get mad, run back into our yard and yank me right back with her. *Ouch!* She did this over and over and over again. I trusted her every time she invited me into the road...and every time the same thing happened.

The day came when she coaxed me into the road again and it was a breakthrough for me. I wasn't going to play her little game anymore.

"Come here Jackie," she said in sweet invitation, but this time I didn't go. I wouldn't go. I knew if I went that she would just jerk me back into our yard again. The only way she could teach me to stay out of the road was to make it so unpleasant that I would no longer want the experience of it.

Later when friends came by and would say, "Hey Jack, come here," I wouldn't go. I refused to go into the road ever again. Our friends eventually learned to come over to the side of the road to see me. I think they learned that they really shouldn't be in the road either.

Sometimes in life our master will teach us and then test us like this. He will send the same painful circumstances to us over and over again until we no longer want what isn't good for us. He will not cease until he is sure that we have learned what we need to know so that he can move us on to new kinds of lessons and experience.

Being in love changes everything. It can override the strictest of rules. You can totally lose your mind when you are in love because in those moments of loving nothing else seems to matter.

There was a little coyote girl who moved into the neighborhood. She was so pretty! We were both the same age and about the same size. She teased me, taunted me and flirted with me.

Her family den was on the vacant lot down the road around the bend. Sometimes when Kate wasn't looking, coyote girl would stroll by and gaze seductively at me. I would sneak out of the yard to go with her. She seemed to know where she wanted to take me and she drew me like a magnet, like a moth to a flame.

All of a sudden I would hear Kate calling from the distant corners of my mind. Her voice might cause me to falter for a moment but the coyote girl was the stronger pull. Kate knew very well I was being courted. Whatever the reason it apparently wasn't a good one. When I didn't come when she called, she would chase after me at breakneck speed, screaming "Jack! Jack Come!" 'JAAAAACK!" Her scream would terrify me. I could feel the desperation in it. The adrenalin.

The fear. By the time she got to me, near that coyote den near the bend in the road, I would be shaking, frozen in my intimidation of her. I would shrink, cowering to the ground. I was so afraid of her when she was like this.

She would make it very clear that she was my master, my alpha. She wanted me to love her; she wanted me to fear her. She was in her strength at these times even though she was sometimes in her pajamas. The most important thing to her was that I was safe, sound and obedient. Eventually we would turn and walk home; me with a humble droop in my tail to let her know that I knew she was boss.

Years later the coyotes would howl from the dark spaces around our house. Kate would command, "Get up on the porch!" It was kind of like a game. We would dash up onto the porch together where it was safe and where we would sit and listen to the coyotes howl.

I would always wonder if coyote girl was out there in the shadows.

I wanted to understand everything about my master. I wanted to know what she wanted of me and I wanted to write it right into my heart. I also wanted to be able to share with her the things I knew that she didn't understand.

Dogs are fully capable of developing a vocabulary but it's not really the words we understand so much as the spirit in which they are said. When she talked she often used her hands as cues, which prompted me to understand more than I would have otherwise.

She talked to me a lot. When she left the house she would always tell me where she was going and when she'd be back. She would ask me to take care of the house while she was gone. She never left without saying "I love you."

I learned a lot of English from her although the language can be very confusing. There are many words that sound the same that mean totally different things. Examples: Wait. Weight. B. Be. Bee. C, see, sea. Herd. Heard. I recently discovered the amazing difference between Heel and Heal. Rough and Ruff! And why when people write words do they capitalize 'I'? Why not capitalize 'You' too? For You are as important as I am. It's hard for me to understand the human ways.

Another word that doesn't make sense to me is the word "dumb." Just because you're "dumb" doesn't mean you're dumb. And vice versa. "Dumb: Lacking the power of speech."

We animals speak with our thoughts not our tongues. We communicate in pictures created in our minds not in sentences made of words. The only reason an animal is "dumb" is because he can't speak in human tongue. In fact, the animals that seem the 'dumb'est are often the smartest! That's why the so-called experts say that Afghan Hounds are dumb. Most Afghan Hounds are so extremely intelligent that they simply can't be bothered with mundane everyday details. There are people who are like that. They can calculate remarkable scientific formulas in their minds yet they won't do things like balance their checkbooks or pay their bills.

No dog is dumb and every dog has a talent. Every single dog has something to offer and, at the very least, a lot of love to give.

Like words that sound the same but are opposite, sometimes I couldn't tell if she was laughing or crying. They kind of seemed the same. I would have to look very carefully at her eyes and her mouth. I assessed the tilt of her head and her breathing pattern. I got quite good at deciphering her but sometimes when she was laughing, tears would come out of her eyes. Humans are strange that way. They live such a dichotomy.

Even though I could hear certain things from several miles away, I am not sure I always used my ears to listen. My ears seemed to be on my head but I think they were located closer to my heart because that's where I would hear the most important things. Maybe they were actually inside my heart, I don't know, but the word "ear" is in the middle of the word "heart" and the word "hear" is heart without the "t" so I guess anything is possible. It's hard to explain but sometimes I could hear a voice somewhere inside my being. It wasn't my voice. It made me think that, like my ears, God was inside of me too.

There were two words that always made perfect sense to me. She and I read a number of books on the subject. These words are the word GOD and the word DOG. We are the reverse of one another it is true. We are opposites. The God-Dog reversal is no mistake because there are no mistakes. What do you see when you look in a mirror? You see the thing backwards. I am purely God's reflection.

A dog always knows what his Master wants and he proves this through his loving obedience to his master on earth. There are mirrors everywhere in life reflecting what we need to see and understand.

My Friend,
I see you in everything
For you're a part of me.

I worship and obey you.
I put no one else before you.
God sent me to you so you can know
How loyal and true He is to you
So you can grow.
While you teach me obedience to you,
I teach you obedience too.

~~~~~~~~~~~~~~~~~~

"Be of one mind," our Master says "and by doing so you'll live in peace."

Dogs speak telepathically. We come here knowing how to communicate with each other. Every dog is fully capable of understanding the pictures in one another's mind. It's how our Master speaks to us, and it's how we speak to each other and to the humans who matter most to us.

When I obeyed her commands I listened to her words, but we communicated best when I listened to her heart where no words were necessary. I had to cultivate patience with her. I would try to broadcast my thoughts to her but she seemed to think that they were her own thoughts. She would cast them aside not knowing that they were my thoughts; not knowing they carried for me great weight and meaning. She seemed to think it was her own imagination but it was actually that I was "talking" to her on the thought waves between us.

Even so, she seemed to want to understand me as much as I wanted to understand her. She wanted to learn what made me tick. She would come down onto the floor with me to see things from my perspective. She would jump up onto the bed and lie around with me on the rugs and play with me like she was a dog too. She would imitate everything that I did because she was trying to figure out how it felt for me to be "me." She'd chase after the ball or the stuffed animal and bat it around like she had paws too. I never saw her so happy than when she was doing that with me. It's like in those moments she forgot who she was. She forgot everything else that mattered in the world. I wasn't sure sometimes if she was playing with me or if maybe she wanted me to play with her.

She had a hard time accepting that we were very different from each other emotionally. While a dog has feelings to an extent, most of us don't really worry about things like people do. We don't fear anything emotional. We don't fear the future. We live in the moment where there is no fear. We have nothing in the future to prepare for. We only experience fear when something physically threatens us or startles us. Once in a great while we can experience a form of fear when we pick up on the emotions of our loved ones and on some level we react to the fear that they feel.

It might seem like we have deep feelings because we look guilty or ashamed when we are caught getting into trouble. We don't really feel guilty because deep down inside we know we are innocent. We live from love and we do the best that we can. When we seem guilty, we have just learned to give you the reaction we know you want from us. You want us to feel guilty? Okay, we can show you how guilty we are. As soon as we do, you stop yelling at us because you then believe that we understand our error (which we usually don't). You might then feel sorry for us because you "made" us feel guilty and then you cover us with your beautiful forgiveness. The game is totally worth it for us to get your love and your forgiveness.

Most pets live in the moment where fear does not exist. Grady was a bit unusual because she had baggage that she brought with her that reminded her that she had a past. If you have a past it can come back to haunt you and then you must therefore have a future...and that's what Grady worried about. She's the one who taught Kate that some dogs worry about stuff, but most of us don't.

Kate would be getting ready to go somewhere. Grady would shiver and shake with apparent fear or anxiety. Kate would then feel sorry for her. She would hug her and coddle her and say, "It's okay little girl; everything will be all right. Awww. You are such a good girl. I would never ever abandon you." It went on and on, the long sickeningly sweet stream of attention. Grady learned that if she started shaking and quaking that she would get a whole lot of love and hear that she was such a good girl! She was no dummy and she was not being manipulative either. She was just playing the game that Kate had created by responding to her that way.

Some dogs bark more than they should; when it isn't necessary or appreciated. A lot of the time when they bark they get the full attention of their master. Just like feeding into a human who complains all the time, giving a dog attention when it barks only encourages more barking. Some owners use shock collars or cut out a dog's voice box. A good master will train a dog early. He will go out of his way to praise his dog in the quiet times for being a good quiet dog.

Dogs don't have a complex emotional life but we can be very sensitive to the emotions of those we love. I could always feel tension mounting in Kate long before she expressed it. Sometimes she would try to hide it. When she would think one way and act another, like pretending she wasn't bothered by something when she really was, it was quite puzzling.

She dated a guy for a short time. I tried to be nice to him but I didn't really like him, which surprised me because I like everybody. I gave him the benefit of the doubt that maybe I was just jealous that he might try to take my place with her. I just didn't trust him. I could smell out his thoughts and what I really didn't like about him was that his thoughts were very different from his words and his actions.

He seemed to like me enough. He would pat me on the head and say, "Hi Jack. Good boy, Jack," superficial stuff like that. She would brag about me to him, telling him how smart I was. How fun I was. He would laugh at her and minimize me. He once referred to a classic cartoon he saw years ago where a man was talking to a dog using big words and what the dog simply heard was 'Blah blah blah blah, Fido, blah blah.' Wow, I couldn't believe he said that right in front of me.

I also was thinking about mirrors and I thought that maybe if I was jealous of him, maybe he was jealous of me too. He never understood the relationship she and I had and he never would. That's why I was really glad when they weren't dating anymore. I think a man who wouldn't try to understand me also wouldn't try to understand her.

Some dogs get very aggravated with people who think one way and act another. We try very hard to read and understand but when someone does not seem authentic it makes it incredibly hard to trust them.

Why do so many people hide? Why can't they all just be themselves?

Weighing in at ninety pounds, I had a lot of hair that made me look even bigger than that. People would ask if I was an Irish Wolfhound, one of the biggest dogs on the planet.

My size scared a lot of people who had little dogs. We would all be out walking and they would jerk and pull their doggies close to them to protect them from me. I was leashed and well disciplined. I would wag my tail and say "Hi!" but the little dogs would bare their teeth and snarl and bark their heads off as if to scare me. It was all such a silly game. Kate would say to me, "It's okay. It's their problem, not yours."

Sometimes dogs just feel the fear of their owner. The fear and adrenalin pulse through the very leash that connects them. It makes otherwise friendly dogs act out of character in an effort to be faithful to their fearful masters. The dogs don't seem to realize that by barking and snarling they actually reinforce their owner's fear and validate their own anxiety. It is a vicious cycle.

It's the same thing with dogs that are aggressive or insecure. They are often reflecting the aggression and insecurity of their owners. It is not their fault. A dog can easily smell whether another dog is vicious or not, but when emotionally complex humans become part of the equation, things can get complicated.

Our friend Sidney was a great dog. He was a shepherd-collie mix and the first year of his life he was badly mistreated. Our friend Stacy rescued him and gave him a very stable life. She was a good master.

One day Kate and I met Stacy and Sidney at a friend's house for a picnic. We had a great time playing and laying around together in the yard all day. Before we went home, we stopped next door to see the neighbors. The kids there were having so much fun in the driveway with their bikes and trikes and jump ropes! It was actually feeling kind of stressful so I stayed pretty close to Kate who was talking nearby to the lady who was the mother of the kids.

The fun stopped abruptly when Sidney snapped at the oldest kid on his scooter. The kid had been roaring at Sidney, pretending to be a lion. Everyone recoiled and said that Sidney was the dangerous one; that he should be 'put down.' Didn't they know it wasn't his fault?

I don't know what happened to him because I never saw him again. I did hear, however, what happened to that family. The mother went into a women's shelter to protect herself from her own husband. Some years later when they were young adults, two of the three kids ended up in jail. The other went to the hospital for an attempted suicide.

This kind of family dynamic is very foreign to dogs. We don't understand it because these kinds of things don't happen in pack families. We take care of each other and yes, we even snap at each other at times when it's appropriate, but we would never hurt each other the way people hurt each other.

Some dogs are more sensitive than others. Sidney was basically a good dog. When he snapped at that kid, he didn't hurt him. He was just the kid's mirror. He was overwhelmed, reacting to the stress of a chaotic family. Dogs feel human fear and we sometimes manifest it. When the fear is severe enough or when it is amplified because too many people around us are feeling it at the same time, we don't know what to do with it. We can react with fear ourselves.

They thought the problem was inside of Sidney when Sidney was just reflecting and expressing the problems that were inside of them. They are the ones who needed the help. They were ones who were looking in the mirror when they looked at Sidney.

It would really be much simpler for us dogs if the people involved would take it upon themselves to express their own anxiety, fears and pain so we don't have to do it for them.

On a positive note, I sure enjoyed having fun! One of my favorite things to do each morning was to run and fetch the newspaper. It was always wrapped in a clear plastic bag and I would grab it and run with it all over the yard! It was great fun, but over time we learned that if we didn't prepare it properly, the paper would be strewn from one side of the yard to the other and the game would be over in no time. I learned to bring it to her first. She would put a knot in the end of the bag and then I would play with that newspaper in the bag for the longest time. It was the bag that made it fun. I could swing it back and forth and throw it up into the air! Eventually she would say "Jack, bring me the paper," and I would run up onto the porch and give it to her. It was a really fun way to start the day.

Driving around town was really fun too. It always made her happy when she saw people smiling in response to me. She'd say "Jack, you light up the world wherever you go." Sometimes when we went into the city the young women and old men would smile and wave at me. The kids and the young men would "Bark! Bark! Bark!" or "Woof! Woof!" at me. Sometimes I would bark back. It was a good time! It felt like we were in a parade or something.

I was sensitive when it came to hunting. I would run my heart out to catch a squirrel but if I caught him I wouldn't have the faintest idea what to do with him. I wasn't a very good hunter because it just was more fun to play the game. From the moment the squirrel arrived on the scene he knew I would never catch him because he knew I just could not climb a tree when all was said and done. I wasn't supposed to catch him anyway because the game was never supposed to end.

My favorite toy was the wacky monkey. It was a toy monkey with a red cape and stretchy rubber arms and legs. She would stretch him and stretch him and then send him flying, like a slingshot. He would land and scream as he landed, a motorized, blood curling scream. "Go get him!" she'd say. I would bound over to him and very carefully and delicately pick him up so as not to hurt him further. I would carry him gingerly over to her and deposit him tenderly at her feet.

My grandmother, matriarch of my Afghan Hound ancestral hunting roots, would have had a fit over my behavior. I never would have made it in my family of origin. Sometimes it's easier to fit into the world than it is to fit into our own families.

Some people just can't seem to mind their own business. Even when you're really well behaved, there are no guarantees. Strange things can happen that are beyond your control.

She must have turned her back for a moment. It was very early on a weekend morning. I was minding my own business, smelling the tufts of grass in the area at the edge of our yard near the road. Lots of dogs would pee along there because they knew it was my yard and they wanted to say hi.

This particular morning a car slowly pulled over and stopped nearby. There was a nice lady in it and her husband was driving. She opened her door and seemed friendly.

"Awww, look at him," she said to her husband.

The lady got out of the car and petted me, asking, "Where do you belong, doggie?"

I belong right here, I said.

"Are you lost?"

No I'm not lost.

She opened the back door of the car and told me to get in so I got in. The door shut and all of a sudden I was trapped in there! They drove me away from her and our yard! They eventually pulled over because they saw one of our neighbor friends walking down the road.

"Excuse me. We found this dog wandering around down there. He seems confused."

If I'm confused it's because I don't know what I'm doing in your car.

"Do you know who he belongs to?"

Kate. I belong to Kate. My name is Jack. Look at my tag. Call her. She will come and get me.

"Yes. That's Jack, Kate's dog," was the reply. "Why don't you take him up there to Lois's for now. She can call Kate to come and get him."

Why don't you just take me home now? Can't you just take me back where you found me?

Lois was one of our best friends. She knew me well enough to know that I would never leave my property; that I would never leave Kate. They told her that they found me 'wandering around' at the edge of the road.

In my own yard, I might add.

Meanwhile in the distance I could hear Kate whistling for me and calling for me. "Jack!" "Jack come!" "JAAACK!" She sounded desperate. Nobody else seemed to be able to hear her but me. She sounded like she was crying. It felt like panic. I felt helpless because all I could do was listen to her. She went all over the neighborhood looking for me. She even went to the coyote den. Later she told me that she was afraid she had lost me forever!

She eventually called Lois, crying, "I can't find Jack anywhere!"

"I know," said Lois, "he's right here."

It was all so confusing. When she came to pick me up she hugged me and hugged me and was crying and pouring her love out all over me. I think that was the day when she first started to worry about losing me.

In the book of Proverbs it says, "A righteous man regards the life of his animal." You can tell a lot about a man by the way he treats his dog.

One of our friends was a handsome Rottweiler. His name was Rox. His owner put a spike collar on him and dragged him around on a metal chain. He would jerk him around in an effort to show him Who's Boss. I think the guy probably treated his wife that way too.

I don't know what makes a person feel they need to control another being. I think they don't realize how powerful they are and how they can utterly destroy someone loyal who loves them. You can tie a dog to a post and demand that it love you, or you can simply love your dog. Your love can be stressful or it can be sweet, the choice is up to you. It speaks volumes about you which choice you make. Your dog will love you either way.

An owner who can't love or accept a pet for what it is must also be a person who cannot love or accept himself for what he is. No one can treat someone or something better than they treat themselves. Once again the mirror looks back at them. The mirror always tells the truth. They never feel safe because they always have an enemy. They think the enemy is you but the enemy is them. They are their own enemy. One can only imagine in the deep darkness of night how they must feel about themselves.

I think the guy just needed someone to control, whether it was a woman or a dog, or both. I got worried for Rox the day he told me that his master's wife was leaving him. I did not like the idea of Rox being left alone with that man.

Some time later we saw Rox at the vet clinic. He was only four years old but he looked fourteen. He died a few months after that. I think under the circumstances that he was lucky to be able to take his leave so that he could fly free in his loving forever home in the heaven beyond Rainbow Bridge. Maybe he will get to come back as a new puppy and have another chance at love on earth. Godspeed Rox.

We are all just love. All dogs, all humans, all creatures. We remember who we are in the depths of our soul and we remember who you are too, but humans tend to forget. They can get off track. Sometimes they don't even love themselves! Humans are emotionally complex, especially when they have been deeply hurt and feel they need to constantly protect and defend themselves. Love can be a frightening experience for people who have been wounded or abandoned by someone they have loved.

How do you see us? Are we your best friend? Are we a scoundrel? Are we the dog from hell? Are we beloved? Are we resented? We are only what you think we are. If you believe we are love, we are love. If you are convinced we are hate, we are hate. We are simply your mirrors. We always reflect back to you what you believe you are.

"I see how you look at me," spits the hateful man. He thinks we look upon him with the evil eye when we are not looking at him that way at all. We are just looking at him. It's because he can't accept the hate inside of himself that he projects it onto us. I don't think the man knows that he does this; it is just a form of denial.

It gets confusing and crazy making. Many humans are trapped in a hall of mirrors. It's important to try to understand why people do cruel and unloving things. They have obviously lost sight of who they are and where they came from. They have obviously lost sight of love.

At the other extreme are people who put their pet first. Whatever the pet wants it gets. They put the pet in control because these people have lost a sense of control in their own lives. They find themselves building their lives around their pet; putting the pets needs before their very own. Cats are adept at taking on the role of running their household because they are typically confident and aloof. A dog will step into the position if no one else is willing to takes a leadership role. Every time the dog begs they feed. Every time it barks they praise. Every time it wants to run they let it off the leash because they want their dog to be "happy". These dogs are not happy; these dogs are spoiled. I looked this one up: "Spoil: To harm the character of; to diminish or destroy the value or quality of."

Some people try to put themselves in our shoes but they cannot. They can only project who they are onto us. We are the mirrors that show them that they are the ones longing for freedom. They think: "If it were me, I wouldn't want to be in a crate!" "I don't want to be fenced in." "I want to be free!" They think: "If it were me..." but it isn't. It's their pet. People are so into free will, but the day their dog runs into the road and gets hit by a car because they didn't want to fence him in or keep him on a leash, they will pay the price of allowing the freedom that they themselves are seeking.

We need to feel safe and secure. We need the same kind of space parents need to give their children as they grow, so they don't grow too fast the wrong way. Clear expectations and boundaries create healthy and well-adjusted adults and healthy and well-adjusted pets.

Many people easily forget how young a dog still is when it looks full-grown. They expect us to act like responsible adults while our brains and maturity lag far behind.

We knew of a large breed dog who chewed up things in the house while her owner was away at work all day. It was no unsurprising behavior. She was 18 months old, the lady had even named her "Chewy" and she was still just a puppy. She couldn't help chewing and she never had any training. The lady didn't even begin to deal with it; she just complained how awful her dog was. I don't understand why people like this don't just get a doll or a stuffed toy instead of a living, breathing animal with needs and feelings.

When the lady owner surrendered her dog she reported, "My dog is a threat." She was lying, covering up for her own irresponsibility. She would rather blame the dog than look at herself. Her dog was not a threat at all. Her young high-energy dog was simply alone and bored all day. The dog needed training, exercise and acceptable things for her new teeth to chew. A mirror always tells the truth. The lady is the one who needed the help.

Many times if a dog is reported to authorities as being a 'threat', it will be euthanized almost immediately. People need to be careful what they say and how they say it. Can you believe that lady went out and got another dog and apparently is complaining again of the very same thing?

Please understand: We are not a threat if we are wagging our tail. That is how we let you know we love you. We honor you. Our tail tells you everything you need to know if you will only pay attention.

We are laughing when it wags. We are afraid when it curls under and hides between our legs. We are crying when it droops and hangs. We are scanning for signals when it is raised like a flag in the air that alerts its troops. When we roll over and expose our undersides, we are surrendering. We are letting you know that we are wholly and truly yours. We are at the total mercy of our master.

I was blessed to have boundaries and a certain amount of freedom within those boundaries. I came to think of her as my beloved, my friend and my master. She never referred to me as a dog. She always called me her best friend or just "Jack".

I knew that she would give me everything and anything but there wasn't anything I wanted that I didn't already have. Whatever my master wanted came first. It was not a sacrifice at all. It was only love, the only law I lived by.

"Only a very evolved being would suppress his own hungers and desire in order to obey his master," she would say. I think she overestimated me and yet it was true what she said about me.

I learned to accept that everything happened in her time. When you live in the moment it's easier to wait. When you trust and have faith you just know that whatever it is will come when it will come. Your master will always bring everything to you at the perfect time.

As I grew I had learned to set what I wanted aside. My desires were less important to me than hers were. I trusted her. I knew she had my best interests at heart. She was very smart and I knew she loved me too. As my master I knew she would always do what was right for me and I knew the best thing for me to do was to follow her commands. I wanted to go wherever she wanted us to go and I knew she would always be beside me. She was my master and I adored her so whatever she said was always *Okay* with me.

"We have to be on a leash in this place."

Okay.

"Stay on the blanket."

Okay.

"Eat your breakfast."

Okay.

"I'll be home soon. Stay home. Take care of the house."

Okay. Okay. Okay.

"The vet says you have to wear this lampshade on your head."

Okay.

"Hey Jack. Do you want to hear about the Big Bang?"

Okay.

I enjoyed the time she read out loud to me about the Big Bang Theory. It was very interesting. With my limited understanding what I think happened was that God decided to play a fun game. He created a great experiment and BANG and Kapoof! He exploded into millions of trillions of little pieces and they are each one of them us, scattered all over the universe. This would mean that we are all pieces of each other. We all belong to each other. I am part of you, you are part of me, always have been, always will be. If you put us all together, well, maybe that is God. Maybe the ultimate goal is for all of us to be together someday, at Home where we belong.

It was getting to be time to step it up a bit. We enrolled in Agility Training. I had lots of fun running fast through the tunnels, jumping through hoops, racing up and down ramps and beams and weaving through small spaces. The other dogs in the group were lots of fun to be with. I'm not sure I was ever competitive enough to win or to even want to win. I was happiest just having fun and seeing others succeed. Kate would smile at me and say, "You get the prize, Jack, for being the most well-rounded and lovable!"

One fateful day, I ran onto the blue and yellow striped teeter-totter for the first time. Going up was a cinch, but it took me by complete surprise when it moved beneath me and crashed to the ground on the other side. I jumped off and I never got back on again. After that I didn't trust walking on manmade structures like planks, ramps, and manhole covers. There wasn't a bridge in existence that I would cross. I was afraid the whole thing would fall out from under me and then where would I be? It kind of ended my agility career. She said it was okay. She said we needed a break from training camp anyway.

Based on my experience with the teeter-totter, I came to believe that some of us have to unlearn something so that we can be free of fear so that we can do the right thing. I had to unlearn what the teeter-totter taught me. It taught me that sometimes things go out from under you when you least expect it. If you are lucky, you will have opportunities to learn again; to help you realize that everything with blue and yellow stripes doesn't fall out from under you and that bridges will get you to the other side.

One day Kate got us a little wooden bridge for our garden. It was about four feet long and six inches high. She called it The Wishing Bridge. As we crossed over it we would say a wish or a prayer and when we got to the other side the wish would come true. The prayer would come to be. At least that's what she told me. I learned to love the bridge and I went over it every time I went out into the yard. The bridge became my friend.

Soon I was seeing bridges in a whole new light. One day I realized that I wasn't afraid of bridges anymore. It was important to unlearn and re-learn this because there would be a very important bridge to cross one day. It's the bridge all pets need to be ready to cross when their time comes.

Kate accepted a job out of town. We packed up our car with all the stuff she needed and we headed west. She had been told that the agency was "dog friendly." She would not have taken the job otherwise. When we got there we had a rude awakening. The agency was dog friendly, yes, but the building it was in was not. I was not allowed inside the building.

She worked very long days. Despite my constant pleas she told me no I could not stay in our car in the parking garage, although I would have been very willing to do so. I would rather have waited in our car all day long than to wait at home wondering about her.

We shared a ranch house in the country with another lady. Outside there were hundreds of acres of rolling hills with horses and cattle dotting the landscape. Yellow wheat fields had giant oak trees rising out of them with blue skies most days. Inside the house we had a nice big bedroom with a nice low window with a view where I could watch horses and birds and (oh, the agony of it) squirrels.

Another dog lived there with us. His master had her own bedroom and bathroom. She always kept the door to her room closed because she said it was a mess. The dog just wandered around the house and in and out of the doggie door to the fenced yard. I didn't go out very often. I wasn't crazy about the doggie door. I missed my jingle bells on the doorknob at home and I missed her coming to open the door for me. I never really felt at home in the ranch house. I was only there because she was there and I wanted to be wherever she was.

The roommate dog was young and handsome. He was restless most of the time because he was bored just walking around the house all day. He kept picking fights with me. I thought he was just goofing around and when we wrestled I always won. Kate was amazed how he, a big strong alpha dog, would end up pinned to the floor beneath me. I would never hurt him. I was always wagging my tail. It was just a game to me. Kate thought we were just playing around too. She praised me, proud that I could be so gentle yet so strong at the same time. It made me want to pin him to the floor as often as possible to see her so pleased with me. Little did I know he was plotting his revenge.

One day while she was at work he strolled into our room like he owned the place. She always hesitated to leave our bedroom door open but she wanted me to be free, not closed up in our room all day. Here he was now and I was on guard. He never came all the way into our room before. She would allow him to come just inside the doorway but only for so long. I decided to handle it the same way.

I watched him very closely. I stood between him and our bed. All of a sudden he started digging in her stuff in our closet. Her shoes! Chewing things. He found her IPod and headphones and took them up onto our bed and started eating them! At one point he dug all the covers off our bed, which she had so carefully tucked into place that morning. The bed was exposed right down to the mattress. He found our flashlight that we used for our evening walks and he chewed it right up! He even pulled her skirt off of a metal hanger and tried to eat the hanger! Her clothes were strewn everywhere! He dragged her underwear out, leaving a trail of it into the living room. I kept trying to stop him but he would bare his teeth at me; he would claw at me and snap at me. At one point he bit me on the side of my face and I was bleeding. I was hurt. I supposed he was getting back at me for winning all those wrestling matches. I didn't know what to do. I felt ashamed that I did not know how to protect our bedroom from him. I couldn't wait until she got home. I knew she would take care of everything.

When she arrived home we were waiting for her.

"Hi guys," she said cheerfully, "how was your day?"

Her smile faded as her eyes gravitated to the trail of underwear. Our things were strewn about throughout the house. At first she looked confused. I just stood there with her, waiting for her to see the rest of it. He was just standing there too. She pushed the door to our bedroom open and the place looked like it had been ransacked, for it had been!

Then she got really mad. She yelled at the dog and he cowered from her, showing his true colors. He slinked away out the doggie door. She looked at me and saw the gash on my face. She cried. She said, "You are too much of a gentleman, Jack, you shouldn't be living with bullies." All this time I was upset about not being able to protect our stuff and here she was upset for not having been able to protect me.

She took me into work with her the next day and told them she couldn't work there anymore. We packed up the car and drove back home. She said she was sorry that we had been separated and that I had been hurt. She said it was all meant to happen so that we would know where we belonged; so that we would know we did not belong there.

When we woke up that first morning in our own bed back at home we both thought we had awakened from the same bad dream.

There was a man she loved for many years. She would often speak of him. She met him on her computer. I saw him a few times. He was very nice to me and he seemed to make her happy, to the extent someone else can make someone happy.

One weekend she was really excited because the man was coming to visit us. The day he was to arrive I had never seen the house or her look more beautiful! Later that day, however, she was crying because he didn't come to visit like he said he would. He didn't even call her to tell her he wasn't coming.

I didn't understand why she was so upset because when someone who loves you tells you they're coming, they will come around, eventually. You just have to say, "Okay" for what else is there to do?

Don't worry. Life is like a dog. If you would only stop chasing it, it will come to you.

She couldn't hear me. She buried her face deep in my fur and cried for his not caring. I think she longed for him more than she loved him. She would look at me and see my loyalty and my undying love for her and then she would cry even more! She tried to make him her everything but you can't make someone your everything because when they are gone you have nothing left.

Only God can be your everything.

When she finally stopped crying about it she could think more clearly. She was talking about him and asked me one day, "How would you handle this if you were me? I just want to do the right thing."

Don't do the right thing; just do the loving thing.

"Wow," she then said, raising her eyebrows, "How would I handle this if he was you?"

She knew she always had the right approach when it came to loving me. That's what unconditional love is. You trust that they love you as much as you love them. You know they never ever mean to hurt you. There is no blame, there is no judgment and there are no expectations.

The day came when she made up her mind to simply accept the man with all of his faults. She just said "Okay," and continued living her life. I was glad she learned the word "Okay." It meant that she surrendered from the fight of trying to control so many things in her life. She stopped feeling so responsible for everything and everyone. I wondered if she learned that from me. I like to think so.

Pets are not capable of taking things personally. This must be why the word "person" is in this word. Pets take and translate everything at face value.

Kate would continually try to put herself into my shoes but the fact is she really couldn't. Like most people, she tended to assume that I would feel the same way she would feel if she were me but it doesn't work that way. I would never take things personally the way humans do. I made no assumptions. I had no expectations. There was nothing that stood in the way of my love for her. Nothing.

"I know there's a person in there," she'd say with certainty, looking deep into my eyes.

Once in a while I would clearly remind her that I was not a *Homo sapiens*, as I eagerly gnawed on a tasty pig's hoof or enthusiastically nibbled every scrap of fat off a bone. I wanted to remind her that I was not a person so she didn't start having unrealistic expectations. I was still just a dog.

I was very sociable. After all, a good manner wins people's hearts and love was the most important thing in my life. I never wanted for anything I didn't have. I never went anywhere I wasn't wanted and I was happy to go everywhere I was invited to go. Life's too short not to make the most of everything!

She would say, "Jack you're so brave!" because I was always willing to try new things and to go out to be with people and their dogs. She's brave too, overall, but there were times when she would be afraid, like when she wasn't sure of herself. I could smell her fear. Sometimes when she was asleep and the nightmares would come I could smell her fear then too. She would wake up relieved that it was just a dream, sliding her foot underneath me just to be sure that I was really there.

Sometimes I think she created her own fears in her own thoughts. It's beyond my comprehension how someone's own thoughts can harm, but no matter, I would lean up against her and try to heal her with the warmth of my body and the loving care of my heart. She would find relief and she would be happy again. That was the best part, being happy with her.

In the quiet times at home I would look at her across the room while she was working at her desk. She would feel my eyes upon her and she would look over at me and say point blank, "You know I love you."

I know, I'd say, *I love you too.*

I liked our house a lot. It was very comfortable. There were plenty of places to hang out when she was gone, but my favorite place was on the concrete floor along the front door. She usually left a pair of sneakers by the door and I could smell her feet while I slept. Sometimes I used them as a pillow just to feel closer to her.

She would be gone and the clock would be ticking, echoing through the quiet emptiness of the house. Meanwhile my internal clock would always seem to know when she would be coming back. Like my role model heroes, Lassie and Hachi, we pretty much know when that train's going to come. We can guess when the car will pull into the drive. If you stay real quiet and focused you can feel where they are. You can feel when they feel they are almost home.

She was working for hospice. She was learning about life by teaching others about death. I got real good at staying home but just like it is with people; pets are healthiest when they are happiest. You can spend only so many hours at home alone. She knew I needed more in my life. She knew that I needed work to do to feel fulfilled. The obedience and agility training had been my work but those programs had come to an end.

She started taking me everywhere. I would go to work with her. We would visit sick people at home and people in hospitals and nursing homes. All day long we would give people attention and love. It made me so happy because that's the reason I came into this life.

At the local nursing home I would go in wagging my tail, ready to go to work loving everybody! In every hallway there would be people with smiles and outstretched arms. One of my favorite nurses would squeal from all the way down the hall, "Is that Jack? Jack! My Jack is back!"

I went there to love them and all they did was love me in return. I think I got a lot more out of it than they did. They received the love of one dog and his master and we were given the love of hundreds.

One day a patient, who didn't seem to be sick at all, asked her if he could take me for a walk down the hall. She handed him my leash and looked at me as if to say, "He needs you to do this."

We walked up and down the hallway and up and down and up and down again. Each time he pulled harder and harder and soon he was dragging me behind him. I was scared of him and wanted to get away from him. It was like he was mad at me but I didn't know why. The more I resisted the madder he got. He was grumbling and then growling.

"C'mon!" he roared through clenched teeth as he dragged me along. Kate stepped in to help me but he shoved her out of the way. He tried to go out the door with me but the door was locked and he got mad at that too. The nurse finally came along with a cup and some water.

"Walter, here. It's time for your pills."

He dropped my leash when he reached for the cup of water.

Kate said she was sorry I had to experience that. She told me that Walter was sick; that Walter couldn't help how he had treated me.

I guess that's what "therapy" is; accepting someone else where they are and loving them anyway.

There was a lady we met who lived at home and her dog was in rehabilitation. Usually it's the other way around. At the age of 15 the dog was learning to use training wheels. His hind legs had failed him.

"He's not in pain and he wants to live," the lady said.

How does she know when she projects her own feelings onto the dog? She feels that if she were in his situation, she wouldn't want someone to give up on her. She feels that if it were reversed, the dog would do the same for her; but she is not a dog and he is not a person.

It might've been different if he wasn't so old. Us pets get tired too when we are later in years. In this case he was the equivalent of 85 years in people years. He had been declining for quite some time. His energy was running low. The fact is, when dogs are ready to go, they are ready to go. They will hang on however, if that's what their master wants them to do. They will even try to learn how to use training wheels.

I hope when my time comes that Kate will be willing to let me go. I don't ever want to end up like these other dogs.

Most pets are very adaptable. They adjust to new lives and quickly learn to love new masters. A few of them however, the ones treated and honored as if they are almost human, have a harder time of it. They are more evolved. Some become so deeply interwoven with their master that they become attached and can no longer imagine living life any other way.

Martha was a youthful 95-year old. She had a black cat named Midnight. We would all hang out together during Kate's hospice visits to see Martha and we all became fast friends. One day Martha took to her bed and she never got up again. Midnight was right there on the bed beside her as she had been for 16 years. Kate offered to adopt Midnight. After all, the cat would soon be in need of a good home.

"No," the family said, "we are going to put Midnight down the day Mom goes."

Kate couldn't believe that they would put a perfectly healthy cat to sleep. She didn't understand like I did that the cat was Martha's friend, pet, partner, soul mate, everything and Martha was the cat's everything too. The cat would have no identity once Martha was gone. The decision had been made.

Like the cat who finds her way back home over a thousand miles, like the dog who waits for his master to arrive on the train that never comes, like the one who keeps a vigil at her master's grave until she too can cross the bridge, some people and their pets are woven together by threads of life and they cannot, and will not, for long be separated.

Sometimes when the chemistry is right we connect easily with someone and sometimes we don't connect at all. It's no one's fault. It's just the way it is. It's nothing to take personally.

Sheila had been blind from a very young age. She lived alone with a housekeeper and her guide dog, Morgan.

I connect with people by looking into their eyes. It was very hard to communicate with Sheila because she wore dark glasses. I couldn't see her eyes and she couldn't see mine. She couldn't see but she knitted, crocheted and she even played the piano. She had alarm clocks, watches and appliances that talked to her.

Morgan greeted me with a pleasant reserve but she took no real interest in me either. I had to admire her. Her soul purpose was to serve her master. Morgan had been trained as a puppy to be a great service dog, and that she was.

We only went to visit them that one time because Sheila said she didn't need me. The only dog she wanted was the one she had at her side. She also didn't need Kate.

"I have everything I need, thank you."

Our ability to connect with other dogs starts in the nose but our ability to connect with people starts in the eyes. We need to see man's eyes and he needs to see ours to be able to fully communicate.

There was a man we went to visit at the nursing home. When we got there he was sitting in a wheelchair facing the wall in the corner of the dayroom. We went over to him and I looked up into his eyes but they were glazed over. They weren't seeing anything. I didn't know how I could possibly help him.

Kate leaned in and put her arm around his back.

"Edward," she said, "Jack is here to see you."

Edward didn't respond.

"Jack is here, Edward. He came here special, just to see you."

Edward's hand was hanging limply off the front arm of his chair; dangling right near my face. I did the only thing I could think of to do. I nudged my head under his hand until his hand was resting on top of my head.

He then lifted his eyes slowly to meet mine. His hand reached out and, almost in slow motion, he ruffled the hair on top of my head. The corners of his mouth curled up into a slight smile. You could tell he was very tired and that this took a lot of effort for him.

Almost as soon as he reached out, his hand dropped back to the arm of the chair. He retreated and was staring at the wall again. They say it was the only time he made eye contact with anyone or reached out for anything while he was there, and it was with me! I heard he died later that week.

Edward. I am glad I met him.

We went to visit a family who had an elderly father at home. They had an old dog that was sick too. Her name was Blanca. I looked into Blanca's eyes and I saw so much sadness there. It was more than sadness; I can't come up with an English word for it.

While Kate talked to the man and his family, I talked with Blanca. She told me that she was ready to cross over but that her master had begged her not to leave. Her master was asking her to stay, so she was staying. A dog is obedient above all else.

I learned that Blanca felt totally helpless. She was tired of living. She wanted to be free of her cumbersome body. She felt trapped. She loved her family but she suffered from a deep and painful longing to return Home. Her heavenly Master was calling for her but her earthly master was clinging to her. It was painful for her to be pulled in two different directions. She knew that I would understand. I felt very bad for her. I hoped that I would never have to live that way.

Our greyhound friend Nellie was turning 16 and was wasting away. Nellie was alert and her tail was still wagging. Like Grady, she was still gracious and beautiful even into her late years.

We went to see her and her master. Kate sat with Nellie. She spoke lovingly to her and tried to heal her in the moments we had together. Later when we were leaving, in the privacy of our car, Kate cried about it. She cried for Nellie and she cried for her master. She felt Nellie's helplessness and discomfort. She felt her master's heartache. She was overwhelmed by the feelings that she imagined they all had. I just watched her knowing she couldn't hear me saying:

Don't cry. It'll be okay. Don't cry it's only life.

For all she had learned working with people and for hospice, she still would forget. She would forget that God was in charge. She seemed to think that she was in control of things.

Why are people so afraid of death? Why do they avoid talking about it? Maybe it's because there are no words. With my limited knowledge of the English language, there is not a word I have ever heard that accurately describes what "death" is. You can look it up in the dictionary for yourself. I don't believe what they say it is. How can you say death is death when it is not death at all, but life?

Our bodies would sometimes get very stressed during those days, doing so much healing work with sick people all day long. After work we would often sit together and talk about our day. She would lay her hands on me. Her hands would travel around my body until she found the hot spots. My head was hot a lot, like a car's engine gets hot, racing for too long. She would put the hollows of her hands on my hotspots and imagine cool waters pouring forth out of them to soothe me. She would be so pleased when her efforts were successful. My hotspots were cooled indeed! Little did she know that I was the one doing the healing. My heat was the healing force.

Heat always goes to the cool, not the other way around. It's okay. Healing was taking place. I was healing her and she was healing me with her love and her intention to heal.

There was a lady who cared for her elderly husband. One day the lady suddenly got very sick. We were just arriving at their house when the firemen were bringing her out on a stretcher. Her wiry old dog was barking and barking and barking! He had been pushed out of the way onto the back porch and was wailing desperately.

Where are you going? What are you doing? She's my master! Why are you taking her away from me?

He just saw a bunch of strange men in uniforms taking his beloved away from him. While we were there we talked with him and reassured him that everything would be okay.

I wish more people would think to look at things from their pet's point of view and talk with them and reassure them about what's going on as things come up like this. The world would be a more peaceful and understanding place.

I noticed she was getting kind of cranky. It wasn't like her. She was starting to question herself and doubt her intuition. She said that the only right decisions she ever made were choosing Grady and choosing me. She felt that otherwise she had made all the wrong choices in her life. She couldn't see that she was supposed to make those particular choices that now seemed to her to be so wrong. It was all by design. Still, she blamed herself.

There's a reason for everything. Don't be so hard on yourself.

I knew it was getting serious when she drove into the garage one day and put the door down. She hadn't shut the car off yet. She was crying saying, "We can leave this place right now." She looked back at me with tear-filled eyes and heavy heart. I think she meant what she was saying in that moment but I think that she was sick on another level and that is what made her depressed. I think she had been gradually getting sick over a very long time.

I agreed with her that it would be quite good to die at the same moment and walk over the Rainbow Bridge together, but that is not our decision. It is not under our control, nor should it be. I was relieved when she finally turned the car off.

I could feel her energy draining. For all our training, I had learned to honor my boundaries but she had not learned to honor hers. She had simply not known to protect herself while she worked with critically ill and emotionally needy people all day every day. She depleted her own health by giving herself away. She had worn herself down to nothing and there was nothing I could do for her but to stay with her and wait for things to work themselves out.

I used to jump at her and give her little love nips and she used to think that it was cute, but I had to stop doing that. It aggravated her now to no end. She would say, "Stop it! Remember they said in training that any behavior where you use your teeth is potentially aggressive! Just stop it!" It was a very sobering time. We weren't having any fun at all.

I didn't like it when she was mad, even though it was usually about her computer or printer or the garage door that wouldn't go up or down. I know she wasn't feeling good but it took me some time to realize that she wasn't angry with me. I was thankful because I never ever got angry with her.

I learned by working for hospice that you can smell when someone is really sick. It's something in the air around them. It's in their aura. I have smelled it many times during our visits with dying people. Each person has a unique imprinted smell, just like animals do.

I started noticing that she smelled different too. It was very subtle but it made me uneasy. She was exhausted yet painfully restless. At hospice when people got restless they were undoing, unwinding, unraveling everything they had come to be and know and do in this lifetime. I worried for her. I never thought I would love enough in this life to fear the future, but I feared that I would lose her. I feared that she would die. She was changing, kind of like how Grady changed. Where once she was strong, she had become weak and vulnerable.

For a long time she wasn't able to work. I would lie alongside her on the bed and try to absorb her pain. I tried to heal her. After all, I was her dog, I loved her and I was at her service. I responded to all of her commands.

"Jack can you get me that towel?"

"Would you please pick up something-or-other off the floor?"

She always said "please" and she always said "thank you." She always said, "I love you."

She walked kind of like the old ladies at the nursing home. I placed myself beside, in front or behind, wherever it felt right to help her, to guide her. I was consumed with her welfare. Her heart was the one that was beating funny now while mine was sure and steady. Like I had learned from her, I would listen to the ticking of the clock on the bedside and imagine regulating her heart with mine. Then I would rest my head upon her.

I will bear your burdens for you. That's why I am here.

It's a scientific fact that having a pet lowers blood pressure and increases overall health. How do we do this? We take your stress and we take your dis-ease. Have you noticed how dogs will sometimes shake themselves after a long petting session? When you pet us, you think you are doing it for us but we are actually healing you when you are stroking us. Cats are the ultimate healers. They rub up against you when you need support and then they walk away and let it go. They don't hang onto it. They don't let it bother them. They'll just keep coming back to heal you.

We are all here to heal and protect the people that we love, but most of us need to be able to run it off and shake it off, so that it doesn't stick to us. I would take the stress from her and would be able to shake most of it off, but not all of it.

We talked again about Martha's cat. Midnight was ultimately put to sleep the day Martha died. Kate had a hard time with that, but now critically ill herself, she gave similar directives for me.

It is not a decision she made lightly and it's not a choice that most people should probably make, but she was right. We were joined at the hip and the heart and I would not want to live without her. When our Master created animals He designed it so that we would die before man. We need to go first because we cannot live without your love and care. If we lived longer than you, we would not and could not survive. It's supposed to be this way. We also need to cross the Rainbow Bridge before you do so that we can be on the other side to greet you when you get there. We wait at home for you here and we wait at Home for you there. It's just the way it is.

I am sure I could've become a problematic dog. Many a dog can become aggressive simply because they don't have a chance to walk off their energy or to fulfill any kind of mission or purpose. I had my purpose, that's one thing I had. My soul purpose is to love and serve my master. As long as I would live upon the earth, my master would be her and only her.

I would find ways to play games with my life to lighten things up. We had a roommate for a while. His name was Tyler. He lived in the spare bedroom downstairs. We liked each other a lot. Sometimes she would not be able to get out of bed at all. She would tell me, "I'm sorry Jack. Go downstairs and Ty will let you out." I would then go downstairs and knock on Ty's bedroom door with my nose and when he let me in, I would play the game of let me in and let me out, let me in, let me out of his patio door. It was really funny how many times he'd open that door for me to let me in and let me out. And let me in.

It was her worst day yet. She had been in a great deal of pain. She begged for relief throughout the day and into night. It was very upsetting for me to see her this way and not be able to help her.

Please relax. Please. Who taught me that that begging doesn't get you anywhere?

She was not one to ask anyone for help, but when people get desperate enough they will ultimately ask God for help because there is nowhere else to turn. This is all by design. He designs the hard times to remind us that He is there. This particular night she sought Him out and prayed to Him for relief. He was her Master and He had been waiting a long time for her to ask Him for His help. Sure enough, a few moments later she had the relief she sought. Something in those moments changed her life. She looked at me more clearly than she had in many weeks. She dusted off her dream notebook the following morning and wrote: "God should always be our first thought not our last resort."

Not long after that things started turning around and she started feeling better. We would go onto the porch and lay in the sun under our blankets. The days were cool but the sun was warm. I think between God, the sun, and me, we helped her to heal and to prepare to start living a new kind of life.

We found ourselves in a new kind of life, that's for sure. First we lost our house. She had been sick for so long that we could no longer afford to keep it. She had put everything she had into building it for us. After the short sale she got rid of almost everything, keeping only the essentials. It was kind of strange to see the undoing of it all.

We moved into another house with a tiny little yard. It's okay. I didn't care. Home is not a place where I live it's the place where I love and wherever she is is home to me.

"Why?" she asked me, "Why did this happen, Jackie?"

My Sweet Friend...
The things of the world are slipping away.
Our house and material things are gone.
Don't you see you now are free?
Certain things you'll never lose,
And don't forget you still have me.
~~~~~~~~~~~~

Things stabilized, they always do. She was sleeping through the night again. We started walking again. She was making us different kinds of foods that I never had before.

She was surprised how I loved our new diet but I liked it mostly because she was eating it too. She would fix a plate for herself and a plate for me. I was crazy for the carrot pulp.

Her friend Stuart and his family were coming to visit from out of town. She was making my favorite carrot, peanut butter pumpkin bread, knowing she'd have leftovers for us later. She served the bread to them and she made little crunchy cookies for me out of the leftover batter. She never left me out of anything.

Stuart seemed to have a knack for knowing the answers to everything. They were talking and she was catching him up on recent events. She told him about Grady's life and her death. She told him about being sick and about losing the house.

"Now I find myself worrying about losing Jack," she said to him.

"8 years, I think," Stuart replied. "You have him until 8."

That's the day I learned my destiny.

She worried long in advance about losing me. Why do humans do that? They spoil the happy times with sadness over something that hasn't even happened. It started before she ever saw Stuart. Perhaps it even began the day she picked me up from the puppy mill; the day she started loving me.

She defied The Fates. She gave credence to Stuart because he was typically right about everything. At the same time she also felt that if she did everything she could to make life healthy and happy for me that she could bypass the number 8. It was as if she could let it slip by while Destiny was looking the other way. She fed me a healthy homemade diet. She took me to have my teeth surgically cleaned because she was told that it could lengthen a dog's lifespan by several years.

She even stopped using the F word because she knew it upset me to hear it. She switched to "frig" but it had the same effect on me so she stopped using F words altogether. She wanted me to vibrate only with love and happiness and perfect health. She was very careful not to allow me to see her upset or depressed because she knew how that could upset and depress me too. It bothered me that she would hide her truth from me to protect me but I guess it was just her human nature. She did everything in her power to give me a life worth living and she was very successful.

We were both getting stronger. We started going for long aerobic walks at the end of each day. The days were getting shorter again and we could easily walk right into the evening. Sometimes darkness would fall before we arrived home and I would lead her across the fields when there was no moonlight. I was blonde and she could always see me in the dark. She would take my curled tail in her hand and we would walk together, safe and sound, all the way home.

I loved it when she needed me like that and asked me for my help. When someone you love shows their vulnerability, it helps you to know they trust you enough to tell you that they need you and it endears you to them all the more. She knew I needed her and I knew she needed me too. She often thanked me for being the light of her life and I thanked her for being the light of mine.

She returned to work. It did not take long before she was once again working all day and into the night.

Haven't you learned anything?

Long after the office was dark she would go to drop off her written reports. I had been in the building with her many times before. I would go in with her to say hi to all our friends and they'd make a big fuss over me. It was really fun then but everything now seemed different. I always obeyed her but this particular night when we arrived at the office I refused to get out of the car.

"C'mon Jack."

She invited me but I wouldn't go.

"Jack come," she commanded but I wouldn't budge.

"What the heck's the matter with you?"

She gave up, sending me a backhanded wave as she went into the office with her papers. I waited in the car for her. I never got out of the car again at that place. I just didn't like her going in there. I was afraid it would make her sick again.

She eventually left that job. Oh, I was so happy! We ended up taking a cross-country trip in our car to visit her family back at home. We specifically drove because she wanted to take me with her. We stopped at lakes and trails and dog parks all along the way. She was doing it all for me. We learned a lot and shared many memories to weave into the enduring tapestry of our relationship.

I never complained but one weekend she knew there was something wrong. Monday she took me to the vet. They found a mass growing inside of me and I was scheduled for surgery the following day. She reassured me, and herself, that everything would be okay. She said, "You're only eight years old and you have a lot more living to do." She said God wouldn't take me now because I am doing so many good things here on earth for so many people. She said I made the world a better place so why would He take me away from it? Of course He wouldn't, she said, because I was needed here. It seemed a reasonable thought.

That afternoon when we returned to the house, an old friend stopped by to see me. Friends come in all shapes, sizes and colors and this friend was a large green and purple spiny lizard. I had seen him before when I was much younger. He had arrived at the front door of our house during Grady's final days. He just showed up one afternoon and I had great fun chasing him around the yard! I never would have hurt him and he never seemed afraid of me. I think he really just wanted me to know that he was my friend. One day he just disappeared. I missed him but I soon stopped looking for him.

I was surprised to see him again early in the spring at our new house. He showed up inside one morning, lounging around on the fireplace hearth as if he belonged there. I pointed him out to Kate.

"What are you doing in here?" she asked him, not really looking for an answer. Lizard and I, we just looked at each other. She picked him up gently and placed him outside.

Here he was again, showing up the day before my surgery. He was hanging around our front door under the light. We both saw him and she said "Hi Lizzie, where've you been?" like he was an old friend.

Morning came early. Other than Lizard's visit, the day of surgery seemed like any other day. As usual, everyone at the clinic was very happy to see me. "Hey Handsome!! C'mon Happy Jack!" they said cheerfully. The nurses were all around me and I couldn't resist their invitations. I was bouncing off the walls with the fun of it all. As always I looked over at Kate to check in with her and to make sure she was still there and to let her know I love her best. I sent out one quick howl when I suddenly realized that she wouldn't be staying with me.

Oh no! Don't go! Don't leave me here!

Had I not listened to her just a few moments before when she sat with me in the exam room telling me I would be staying here for a little while, that she would be back for me and that everything would be okay? Why was I so surprised that she was leaving? In the chaos that swirled around me, had I lost the ability to hear what I needed to hear?

"C'mon Handsome!"

"Go ahead," she said. "I'll be back for you, I promise. I love you Jack. I love you."

I turned my head and was off and running, prancing down the hallway with my pretty nurse.

Everything was different when she came back for me that afternoon. I was coming off the anesthesia and was pretty uncomfortable. With her gentle encouragement I was able to get into our back seat and she drove us home.

When we got home, all I wanted to do was go upstairs to bed. I stood at the foot of the stairs waiting for her.

"No, Jack," she said. "We can't go up there." She was crying while she said it. "You aren't allowed to go up the stairs."

I just wanted to be in our bed, to be quiet and calm with her...but I could not, by her order.

Okay.

I didn't understand that I wasn't supposed to exert myself. I was dazed and confused. I just wanted to go to bed. I wanted to lie down with her beside me.

She must have read my mind because she set up a big bed for us on the kitchen floor. The whole floor became one big bed. She brought me my favorite pink and blue baby quilt, the one she wrapped me in the day she brought me home from the puppy mill. I loved that quilt; it just got softer with age like most of us do.

The monsoons came in the night. It rained all night and all day for days on end. It was as if the grey clouds had moved in and took the sun from the sky. It seemed fitting, almost comforting.

She stayed home with me. She would not leave my side. She learned to turn and position me so that I would be more comfortable because I couldn't do it by myself anymore. She kept putting the hollows of her hands on me to heal me. She was successful to an extent.

Life went on around us. Cars passed, thunder clapped, storms raged. The phone rang. She usually didn't answer it. She didn't go to work. Lizard was still there. He kept a constant vigil on the stucco wall outside our door. We stayed in our personal vortex of love and hope. Nothing else mattered to either one of us. We were both just living in the moment together.

She prayed that the power of God and her faith would heal me. I kept declining. She asked for help from the sun and the moon and the stars and Jesus and Mother Mary. She asked for blessings from all the apostles and saints and all those who had gone before, to help us. She even asked for help from the Lizard on the wall.

It was simply getting to be my time to go. I felt it. I knew it. Somewhere inside of me I had the willingness to leave. It was like someone was calling me from far, far away. "Come, Jack, Come. Come Home." As much as I loved her I knew I needed to answer the call. I had no choice.

It felt strangely familiar. It reminded me of something that now feels like a dream. I was pursuing the little coyote girl. I heard Kate calling in the distance, "Come Jack! Come home!" I tried to ignore her call. I really wanted to be with the coyote girl but my master's voice was stronger. Now here we are again and my heavenly Master's voice is strong.

I knew then why I had to suffer. The older we get the more reasons God gives us to seek His comfort. In the end He sends us just enough pain and suffering so that we will want to leave. If everything were perfect we would never choose to go. He wants us to seek an end to our suffering because He wants us to want to come Home.

She continued to watch me go downhill. I think it was harder on her than it was on me. Sometimes it's easier to be the one going through it than to be the one watching the one going through it.

The days ran together. She was consumed with trying to control my pain. I kept spitting my pills out. She cried because she felt she needed to give them to me but she knew I didn't want them. She would force them into my mouth, crying the whole time. Yes maybe I was in pain but she didn't know how terrible those pills were!

She called the vet to ask for stronger medication on the third day. I didn't want it but you couldn't tell her anything; she wasn't hearing anything. She asked her friend Suuz to pick up the extra pills from the vet for us. By the time Suuz arrived, I had gone from bad to worse and by then the clinic was closed for the day.

"You have to take him to the hospital, he's not going to make it," she was told.

She was torn. She desperately wanted me to survive. The hospital was a long way away. Kate knew it would be a very difficult trip for me and once we got there she knew that I would be put in a kennel or a crate or something. Yet, looking ahead, she knew that she would want to look back and know that she had done everything possible to help me.

"You have to take him. You have to." One after another told her this.

Suuz simply said, "What would you want if you were him?"

"I don't know," Kate replied helplessly, looking to me for an answer.

Please don't take me to that place. I'm not going to make it anyway. I just want to stay here with you. I just want to stay home.

"If you want to take him, I can help you get him into the car," Suuz said, giving her the opportunity to make that choice.

It was now or never. Once Suuz was gone there would be no one available to help us. Kate would not be able to get me into the car all by herself. She didn't know what to do.

It just so happened that I was lying with my backside along the door that led to the garage. I was resting. She didn't want to move me because she didn't want to disturb me; rest now came so infrequently. She couldn't get into the garage without the garage door opener, which was inside her car, which was in the garage. Even if she had been able to access her car, Suuz's car just so happened to be parked directly outside in its path. They didn't know it yet but Suuz also had a flattened front tire.

Like I said, I don't want to go.

I had been praying to be able to die at home on my own terms.

It was evening and we were alone again. I could relax a little bit. She had come to the realization that there was no hope for my survival. Instead of praying for my recovery, she now prayed only for my comfort. She prayed for sleep to come to me. She prayed to God and the archangels and all those who had gone before. She made sure that I knew that I would not be alone.

She seemed calm but I knew that in her heart she knew that I would be leaving soon. As the night went on she couldn't help but whine and whimper as she tried to comfort me. I knew that she was sad because that's what you do when you're sad. I know. I have whined and whimpered too. You whine when there's something you want that you can't have and you whimper when you know that it's out of your control; that there's nothing you can do about it.

As I got worse I couldn't help but whine on each exhale. It was evidence of my pain. I didn't want to whine because I knew it upset her but I was not able to hide it. I tried. I then understood why she had tried to hide certain things from me along the way. I learned a lot about communication by being with her.

The clock ticked on the wall above us telling us that time was passing, bringing me closer to the end of this journey.

Pets often try to find a private place and time to die alone. We don't want our loved ones to remember us in our dying moments. But there you are on the floor and there she is beside you and you cannot move. You cannot hide. So I made the best of things. Maybe God needed her to see me suffer so she could let me go. She knew I had to leave and that if she clung to me it would be much harder for me. She had worked for hospice long enough to know these things.

I must have become more human in my time on earth because I found myself on that kitchen floor thinking about the future. Mine. Hers. I knew I had become more human because I was self-conscious in my death. When the final moments came I buried my head in my pink and blue blanket so she could not see my face; so she could not see the pain of my leaving her. After all, the last memory often becomes one's first memory and I did not want her to remember me that way. I didn't want the blanket pulled back until the peace had come to my face. The peace that would come from realizing that this new adventure is a good one and that all is well. I was thinking about all of this as I was breathing my last.

I was leaving in my prime and it was okay. I was spared from having to live my life as an old dog. There was never anything I attempted in life that I couldn't do. I had been blessed.

But oh I loved her so! As I was leaving she was weeping, commanding me through her tears, "Go. Go home Jack. I love you. You're doing the right thing. You have to go. Go Home little boy!"

I didn't want to leave her but I was obedient, first and foremost. I knew I had to go Home. She was sending me ...and I was being called.

When I closed my eyes it was black and the next moment when I opened them it was white; it was all light. Black is nothing, white is everything. Everything is nothing. Like the color white, nothingness is everything although it seems like nothing.

It all sounds crazy to you right now but, believe me, it will make sense the moment you come Home. I could see it all so clearly. I could see what it is that we are waiting for. I knew in one solitary moment why I had learned obedience and why I valued nothing on the earth but love. It's all that matters. It is all there is.

A string of flashbacks came to me. My grimy cardboard puppy mill bed...Grady falling into the rose bushes...the dog attack...the weeds and stickers and prickers of life...her tears in my final moments...all of them flashed before my eyes. The painful memories came to say goodbye. They are filtered out of us at the end of life. We cannot take them where we're going because they only weigh us down.

My memories flashed all the way back to a time before I knew her...when love was just a dream; a dream that would come true for her and for me. We take all that love with us and it becomes all that we are.

Life goes on and something is always turning into something else. I now know this for sure: Love is all there is and love never dies. Love is energy and energy does not die; it cannot die. Einstein would tell you that it is a proven scientific fact. If it's energy, it must live, although sometimes it changes form.

Love does not sleep. I am not dead. I am awake.

As I slipped away, before my body got cold, I felt a heat so intense. She felt it too from head to toe. She felt the heat of all the love I felt for her and all the life she'd given me. I tried to take her with me but I couldn't. I planted a piece of me inside of her heart. I did not want her to be without my love, ever!

Thousands of thoughts bombarded me. I could hardly keep up with them. I thought of the sun, too bright for eyes to gaze upon. Yet still we see its light, feel its warmth, and experience how its presence inspires the whole wide world to grow. I now could see the sun in all its glory and feel its warm and gentle welcome.

I thought about water. Water in my dish. Water from the freezer turning into cubes that turn back into water before they disappear. Water in the teapot turning into steam; into vapor. Water boils; steam rises...I had never thought about this before and yet that's what it seems I did. I rose and felt that I turned into vapor too.

"Go home Jack," she was telling me through her tears. "Go home over the Rainbow Bridge. I'll see you on the other side. I promise."

I found myself thinking of and feeling like and knowing about rainbows. Rainbows are made of millions of bits of light and water but they don't really exist. They only exist in a person's vision because the sun hits the mist in a certain way that reveals it to the eye. Rainbows aren't really there at all. In fact you can't even cross over one until you are the same as they are. I'm almost there and all of these thoughts come a thousand times faster than I can share them.

We are on two different frequencies now. That's the only reason she can't see me. She is the water and I am the steam. I rose up and out of my body. I could see everything from every angle. I was each particle and every particle all at once. I was free of pain and while it felt strange to be outside of my body, I felt such peace come over me. It was better than taking a deep and unexpected afternoon nap in the quiet warmth of the sun.

I observed her weeping. "I love you I love you I love you," she kept saying. She lay there beside my shaggy body under our shaggy blanket with her arms around me, holding me and petting me. It was 3 a.m. There was no one to call. There were no interruptions. It was all by design.

There are not enough words in the English language to describe the experience of this. Death is more than life. Humans put their animals "to sleep" when it's really waking them up. Everybody has it all backwards.

The first thing she did when she knew I was gone was to close my eyes but they wouldn't stay closed. So she left them open. She got up long enough to get a wet cloth to clean my face. She stepped outside for a moment to see Lizard to let him know that I had passed. "...But then you probably already knew that," she said to him. Lizard had been there all week long, always in the same spot beneath the light near the front door. Kate had given him daily progress reports: that I was going to the vet, that I was going to have surgery, that I was coming home, that I was getting worse and then, that I had died. Lizard knew I was not dead.

She returned and brought my favorite comb. She combed me for the last time. Two hours later she was still running her hands through my hair, trying to hold me in her memory, every last bit of me. She was living in the moment.

At one point she sat up with a start. What was that? She thought maybe I was still alive! Denial is a powerful thing. She looked at me intently. She could've sworn my eyes were following her. Maybe they were, for yes I was watching her it is true. She put her hand on my heart only to find that she was feeling her own steady heartbeat through me. I was still warm only because my cold body had absorbed her heat.

The light of the new day came into the sky. Our friend Reggie arrived with it. She and I were still on the floor under the shaggy blanket. He came to help us.

"Hey my buddy Jack," he said to me sorrowfully. He was so sad, a big strong sad man. He lifted me up in my pink and blue blanket and placed me in the back seat of our car to wait until the vet opened for the business day.

She made sure my body was comfortable and then went back into the house and worked fast to clean everything up. She cleaned the floor. She washed all the dishes and bowls, the blankets and the towels. She put the pills away and the peanut butter that she tried to hide them in. She picked up my dog dishes and packed them in a box in the garage. She cleaned until there wasn't a trace left of my illness. I was happy about this because I did not want her to focus on my death. I do not want her to think of me as dead. I am not dead!

When she returned to the car, she sat with me. We were both in the back seat, which was still like a comfy den since the day Grady was there. I was glad we never changed it. She took my collar off for the last time. She petted me. She talked with me. Over and over she told me that she loved me. She was amazed that just hours before I had seemed almost ancient, my face stressed with pain...but there I was in the backseat of our car looking beautiful just like Grady had looked that day. I was at peace and I knew that all was well.

It took just a little while for me to understand the journey and to allow the tranquility to come over me. Everything is as it should be.

My Friend...
Please don't judge my death as "bad".
It is not bad. It's just a dream.
It isn't real.
I know that you can't see that yet.
You want me to wake up
But in my death I did wake up
And I saw you were still sleeping.
You thought that I was leaving
But I was just arriving.
Here they all remember me.
They've all been waiting here for me.
They've invited me: "Jack come and play!
This is your home, it's where you'll stay!"
Guess what?
They love me as you do.
Just think, they love you that much too!
If you can just believe it's true,
You will cry no more.

~~~~~~~~~

She drove to the vet clinic and parked outside the big heavy industrial door; the same door where we last saw Grady. She couldn't bear to watch them take me out of the car so she got out and walked away from all of us. I was glad she did. She already had enough memories that she didn't want to remember.

When she got home a little later, she gave Lizard the report that I was gone. He just sat there and looked at her, blinking a couple of times. She went outside to see him again later that night but he wasn't there. She wanted to talk to him. She was missing me and she missed him too. She put the light on so that he might come back to feed on the flying bugs it brought but Lizard did not return. He disappeared after spending every moment of the last week of my life with us.

The next morning after a sleepless night, she went out again, looked for Lizard to no avail and sadly turned off the light.

Some people are so filled with fear they make it a point never to get close to anyone just so they never have to grieve over losing them. It would have been much easier for her if she didn't know me so well, if she hadn't loved me so much.

I continually reassured her. I thanked her for letting me go. I told her that I loved her but she couldn't hear me. She couldn't hear any of it.

Over the days ahead I sent her reminders of me. I sent her clouds shaped like me and trees that whispered my name as she passed by. Then one day she heard my dog tags jingling on the trail. Soon after that she saw my face in the patterns of her curtains and also in the clouds that passed in front of the moon. She thought when she saw these things that she was going crazy but she was not crazy at all. She just didn't realize that the messages were coming from me.

At night she dreamed I came to her but when she woke she remembered only fragments: me, exit doors, entryways, my collar, my tangled leash, the rain. Always the rain. She was still too stressed to put it all together. She didn't even open her notebook.

A week went by. It was raining again when she drove to the clinic to pick up my ashes. She tried very hard to be stoic and to keep a stiff upper lip. She was afraid that if she started crying that she would never stop.

Our friends the nurses crowded around her. They loved me too.

"We're so sorry. We'll miss him too," they said to her.

The veterinarian who did the operation passed through the office, very near to her. She tried to connect her eyes with his but she couldn't. She realized later that he loved me too and that he couldn't bring himself to meet her eyes. He was stoic just like her and for the same reason.

They brought out the urn that held my ashes. She accepted it and held it close.

"It's so strange," she said, "but it feels good, the weight of him y'know?"

She took great comfort in holding me. She was holding me in her arms again although she knew perfectly well that I was not in there. The ashes were all she had left of my body but memories of me were everywhere. We had gone everywhere together. Everywhere she went, I was. Still she clung to that plastic urn of ashes.

I tried to comfort her. I spoke in a voice she could not hear. Her grief and sadness drowned me out. I wanted to tell her what I have always known. That life is but a dream leading to love. Love, more powerful than her fear could ever be. Love cannot be destroyed. It grows and grows until it is stronger than death.

Oh My Friend,
If only you would listen
You would hear my voice inside your heart
Telling you I never left.
Telling you I never will.
~~~~~~

She had a pretty card by her bed that read: "Blessed are they that mourn, for they shall be comforted." Well then, she would say to herself, I guess I am blessed!

It was hard for friends to know how to comfort her. After all, I had been like her child, her boyfriend, her husband and her friend all wrapped up in one package. Pets can become like family members, especially for those who never had a family of their own.

Some cheerfully spoke of memories they had of me that made her laugh and cry at the same time. "Oh that Jack, he was a such honey bunny." They'd cry, "We'll miss him too." Some people told her, "It's only a dog. You'll get over it." Others said, "You'll never get over it." I was glad to hear the dog lovers tell her "He is right there with you." "He lives on in your heart." I hope she heard them because they were telling her the truth.

I watched her on her lonely walks, traveling to places we used to go. She would start out strong and end up withered by her tears. It's hard to imagine how a human can shed so many tears but it's important for them to be able to cry when there is so much sadness inside of them.

I have studied her tears through the years. The human body was designed for joy. It can't contain such sorrow. The heartache leaks out through the eyes and sometimes through the nose. Tears must fall for if they did not, the person would be marooned on an island of sadness forever. Tears flush the heartache away so the person can grow and love again.

Pets don't typically shed tears because we unconditionally accept as fact that which happens to us. We know our Master has designed everything for our highest good well ahead of time. There's really nothing to cry about. That said, once in a great while when certain pets bond and become more like their humans, they can cry too. That's why we sometimes have little teardrops at the ends of our noses. That's how you know that we are affected by the emotions of our beloved.

If I had nostrils there would be tears there now, I am sure of it.

I was glad when she began to walk our favorite forest trails again. It was a positive step for her and being out in nature is good for the soul. At first she cried every step of the way but after some time passed she only cried at my favorite spots.

This particular day I tried to reach her, for there she sat on an old tree trunk at the edge of the western trail. She was crying again because it is a place we used to sit together.

I wish that she could hear me above the chaos of her mind, but my eager words have so far fallen only on deaf ears. Whenever we would go somewhere together there would be many voices all around us; people yelling, dogs barking and sounds of the street...but the only voice I would always hear loud and clear was hers. Now the grief screams and her heart cries and there is no way for her to hear me.

I remember when there was something important we needed to hear we would both get real quiet so that we could hear it together.

"Shhhh! What's that?" she would ask me in a crisp whisper. We'd stay real still and hold our breath and listen.

Shhhh, I now say, don't you cry. If you stay calm you'll hear my voice. You'll know my thoughts. I speak to you most all the time. Please let me calm your aching heart.

Suddenly I came up with an exciting idea. I sent a bolt of lightning out of the clear blue sky. It struck nearby and she stopped crying right away! It was very effective, but soon she was crying again. Then I sent a hummingbird moth to dive-bomb her. It gave her goose bumps and it made her stop crying too, for a little while.

That night she got into bed feeling cold and lonely. She was wrapped up, crying in our blanket, which was still alive with memories.

My Friend,
Cast that shaggy blanket aside
Let me cover you in the warmth of my love.
Do you think that blanket is real
And I am not?
I am more real than any blanket could ever be.
~~~~~~~~~

She surprised me by breaking the long heavy silence in the house by calling out, "Jack, come," as if I were right downstairs. Had she felt my presence? A few moments later she patted the blanket on the bed in invitation like she always did each night with me. "C'mon," she said as if I were right there, and then "Yay!" I could sense that she felt silly calling out for me that way. She was glad that no one could see her. But I saw her. I was there.

She must have felt me there because she warmed up very fast. She removed the blanket and kicked off the bedcovers. Throughout the night she felt my warm presence, like a dream. She continued the game in the morning.

"Come on Jackie, it's time to get up. Let's go!"

She said it all excited like she always did but now she was also crying as she said it.

If only she knew what I know, she would not shed another tear.

She was going through the anger stage. She didn't do it quite like other people do. I am glad that she was never angry with me for leaving her. I am glad she was never angry with God. I wish she knew how proud He was of her for following the master plan.

First she wanted to blame the vet. Maybe he made a mistake. Maybe he could have done more. Then she thought about blaming Stuart for putting the 8 in her head. She even blamed my grain-free diet as she recalled the big dogs from her childhood that lived to be twice my age eating ordinary dog food. She wanted to blame someone, anyone, for her pain and her loss. Why do people feel better when they blame someone? I don't know. Maybe it just feels better to be angry than to be sad.

She ran out of targets to blame and then she turned on herself. "What more could I have done? What did I do wrong?"

She felt that she had been responsible for my life and therefore must be responsible for my death as well. She reviewed over and over what she could've done, what she didn't do, what she should've done.

As dogs we are innocent until proven guilty yet people seem to feel guilty until proven innocent. Why do people do this? Where does all that guilt come from? Don't you see that we are all innocent? Every last one of us! Guilt is so unnecessary. It only makes things more troublesome.

Stuart knew. He knew I'd pass at eight years old and I was three months shy of nine. I am sure that if anyone could have changed the outcome it was she, but no matter how healthy the food was that we ate, no matter how many times my teeth were cleaned, there is an inevitable time and place at which point there is nothing in your power that you can do to change the outcome. In a certain time and place you will simply go in your own way.

Some leave a little at a time like Grady did and some leave all at once. With Grady there was an element of relief that she was finally free; there were positive reasons for her going. As for me she will always say that I was taken too soon. No matter what age, when one loves, it is always too soon. I had said my prayers. I wanted to be taken in my prime so that she would always remember me as perfect. I did not want to be old and infirmed. I did not want to be a burden to her. She will never have to remember me as an old crippled dog.

Grady is a Certified Homebody here. When I first arrived she was the one who guided me in the ways of Heaven. I think she has made the decision to come back as a puppy again. I wonder if she and Kate will cross paths. I have asked her to be patient with Kate for there is still so much she doesn't yet understand.

Several times over the years since Grady made her passage Kate would tell me how she saw Grady in her dreams. In the dream Kate would say to her, "You can't be here Grady, you died." Inevitably as she said that, Grady would disappear, poof, just like that.

I tried to explain to her that she needed to accept Grady into her dreams. She needed to give Grady permission to stay. Until she did, Grady would have to honor what Kate believed to be true. So when Kate said, "You can't be here," Grady could not stay. That's the way it works.

A loyal pet obeys its master even beyond the grave.

Seasons change and life goes on. People die and babies are born. Summer has turned into autumn. Tonight she was walking through the fallen leaves along the side of the road. As she walked she seemed to be accompanied by a big empty hole that was walking along with her in the place I used to be.

You are not alone. I am everywhere you go, I'm on every path you take.

I keep hoping she will hear me but she doesn't. Her progress has been slow but the day will come when she will move beyond her grief. There are stages a person must go through and they can only go through them at the pace that is right for them. Some heal quickly and some take much longer to learn to live with loss.

She remains preoccupied with me, staying up late to read all kinds of stuff about losing your pet and saying goodbye. She has watched every movie there is about dogs and she has cried through all of them. She reads books about dogs, books written for dogs, books written by dogs. There are so many good ones! I think it's kind of funny how many people who write about dogs have the first name of Cat or the last name of Katz. Human life on earth is full of such ironies.

"Pets don't go to heaven," someone carelessly told her. She is strong enough, but some people who are not so strong in their faith are shattered by such words. Those who truly love need the faith that love never ends. They need to believe they will see their loved ones once again in some way, shape or form.

A sympathy card still sits on the desk in front of her. It reads: "In His hand is the soul of every living thing, and the breath of all mankind. Job 12:10." I know it brings her peace of mind and gives her faith that we will meet again.

Dogs don't have the human need to be "right" but I know I am right about this:

We start out in Heaven and, unlike our humans; we never forget where we came from. Even on earth there are many stories of dogs and cats that found their way home against all odds. Time means nothing and no distance can stop our return. We know where we need to be and we know who we belong to. No fear or trepidation can sway us from getting there. We always know where home is and we know our final home is Heaven.

"Oh no," they say. "Dogs don't have souls." Or they say, "Dogs have souls but cats don't." Where do they come up with this stuff?

Ecclesiastes, a friend to all beings, said: "For that which befalls the sons of men befalls the beasts as well. As one dies, so dies the other; yet they have all one breath. A man has no preeminence above a beast, for all is vanity. All go unto one place."

If something breathes it has a soul. Breath is divine life force that comes and goes like the tides. This breath infuses every creature on the earth, in the sky, and of the sea. It is evidence of the very spirit in every last one of us. If it bleeds it has a soul, whether it is a man, an animal or a tree that gives its sap to the syrup.

Life is life. God is life. Soul is the invisible part of a living being that is immortal and breath is the evidence that the soul exists. The soul is what goes to Heaven when we no longer need our body here. We may be animals, but we breathe, we bleed, and we love just like anybody else.

When you are dependent on your master and show your loyal obedience you will find that your master wants to give you everything. In the same way, when you trust your master with faith in all he is and does, you want to give him everything too.

That's how it works. Love is not give and take; love is give and give. When we love we want to give each other all that we have, all that we are, all that we will ever be. This is where love's perfection exists. Once in a great while it can be found in special partnerships on earth, but this love is the norm in Heaven.

My Friend,
I plan to give you everything
That you have given me
And more.

A mandate here in Heaven says:
We're to give what we've received
And return the gifts,
Tenfold!
Oh what fun it's going to be
To give you what you gave to me!
~~~~~~~

I was quickly learning creative ways to reach her. One morning I found a really fun way to send her a message. It was a sunny day but she wasn't really seeing it. She was out on the patio immersed in her thoughts, pondering where her life was going without me.

Out of the blue some guys drove by in a golf cart.

"Hey, is Jack around?" one hollered to a guy walking down the street.

"He's around here somewhere!" was the walker's confident reply.

A slight smile came to her lips.

"Jack," she repeated. "Jack. He's around here somewhere."

Just because you can't see me doesn't mean that I'm not there.

She used to talk to her goldfish. She would become an instant advocate for them when, after introducing a friend to her fish who swam up to "greet" them, the friend would say, "Don't you see, Silly, they are just wanting their food. Fish don't think. They don't have feelings." Kate paid no heed.

She talked to her plants, she talked to her car; she sensed that everything had feelings and she would put herself in their place and try to give them what she thought they needed so that they would be happy; so that they would feel loved.

She didn't realize we already felt loved by the very fact that we existed. She didn't know that she was giving us what she needed. All you really have to do is look at what someone gives to you to know what it is they need from you.

Once again, she was looking in the mirror because she was really the one who needed to feel loved.

That's really why I chose her to begin with.

It's been three months. Time has passed and yet it seems she still is trapped inside her broken heart. Oh the tears! Will she ever run dry? I wish I could help her move through her grief.

She used to sing the Beatles song "Let It Be" to me when life would get stressful for us. It's a good song.

Tonight is Halloween, the day of my earthly birth. She is singing the song, crying tears into the pumpkin apple carrot birthday cake with peanut butter cream cheese frosting that she made for me. She did that instead of going out to the Halloween party that she was invited to.

It is a strange time for a birthday, Halloween, the eve of Dia de Los Muertos and The Day of The Dead. I am gone from her sight yet it is as if she keeps me alive. It's a haunted day to begin with and I have to admit that I feel a bit like a ghost, a phantom; hanging, suspended between birth and death. Dangling between Heaven and Earth is not an easy thing for I am not fully alive in either place.

She worked at the hospital today. People still ask about me and she can finally answer them without crying.

I watched her finish her workday. Her last patient was a man who had lost his legs, now learning to walk with artificial ones.

As she got into her car afterwards, she took a moment to soak in the quiet warmth of the sun. She wrote her progress note about the man with no legs. As she wrote she thought about how fortunate it was that she had legs. She had to admit that even if she didn't have me, most things in her life were very good.

Her mind was in the right place. I thought the time was right to make an attempt to reach out to her:

My Friend...
There can be such pain for some,
When those they love cannot let go.
It's hard to disconnect from life.
It's hard to cut the ties that bind us
To the ones we love.

You know that guy you saw today?
The one with pain in both his legs;
Legs that he no longer had.
You said he suffered 'Phantom Pain',

The pain that comes from staying
Attached to a former part of you
That hurts even though that part is gone.

Listen to the words you say
For you are still attached to me.
You bind me to you with your grief,
Pretending I'm still there with you
Like the man pretends that he has legs.

~~~~~~~

An early snow was falling as she drove up the interstate. She used to talk about getting us a red jeep. She pictured me with my big shaggy head out the window while she drove on and off-road, plowing through the fields and the snow in a rough and tumble jeep. Nonetheless she was still driving her little sedan.

This particular day it was snowing so hard that she had to watch the road carefully. It was not a good day for her to be crying but she was. I was concerned she'd end up in the ditch or across the median.

Please don't cry, I said to her.

She couldn't hear me, no surprise; my voice drowned out by tears that seem to never end.

All of a sudden she did a double take in the rear view mirror. A jeep was coming up fast behind her. Its bold cherry red color was a sharp contrast to the newly fallen snow. It was traveling fast enough to get her attention. As it passed she glanced over with interest. Then quite unexpectedly it pulled into the lane in front of her and escorted her at a safe speed for quite a long time.

Its license plate read: "LETITBE".

Her favorite words of wisdom had made themselves known in a way that she could not deny was God and myself at work in her life.

A few days later she had breakfast with our minister at a local restaurant. She told her the story of the red jeep. Like our friend Stuart, Cherokee has the gift of knowing certain things in the space that separates Heaven and Earth. I reached out to her in the hopes that she could translate to Kate for me. I tried to get inside her mind. It seemed like it was now or never...

Shortly after they placed their order Cherokee looked at her intently and leaned forward.

"There's something I need to tell you," she said to Kate in a hushed tone.

"Yes, what is it?"

"You need to let go of Jack. You are binding him to this earth plane by continuing to imagine him in your life. You need to cut the cord and set him free."

Kate was speechless. Tears stung her eyes. She had never really thought about it that way. She thought I would want her to want me around her all the time. She thought that if she were me that she would want to be missed. She would want to be wanted. But again, she isn't me and that's not how things work in Heaven. In a way she was pretending that I had never left. She was still in denial.

She's right, you know. You haven't let me go. You are still clinging to me.

"Oh my God," Kate replied, "It's like Jack's at the dog park in Heaven and I have him on a leash while all the others there run free. I have done him a great disservice."

She was upset and crying again. Part of it was that guilt-thing, but also she knew it was time to unleash the invisible cord that was woven out of her sadness, loss and longing for me. She had been binding me to her with her grief.

I knew it would be just a matter of time before she would be happy again. Once she was happy then I could be free.

She wrote in her notebook a lot during our time together but she hasn't written much since I crossed over. I have been thinking that she would feel a lot better if she wrote about it.

Tonight she picked up her favorite pen, opened up her notebook and asked me for my help. Wow, I had my chance and it was amazing! My words flowed right out of her pen.

When she went back later to read what she had written, she looked at the words on the paper and said, "Wow. Where did this come from?" It was what I had said to her. This is the moment the concept of this book began. These were the words, my words, she wrote:

My Friend...
I loved you at first sight.
I loved you at last glance.
Look up what Heaven* means
And mourn for me no longer!
For Heaven is where I am...
*(She later looked it up.
"Heaven: God. A state of being eternally in the presence of God after death.
A place, state, or experience of supreme bliss.")

...My new life is amazing.
I now know everything I am
And everything I've ever been.
Without gravity to hold me down,
I move faster than my train of thought.
My own thoughts carry me along.
I think of you a lot and when I do
I'm there with you.

My thoughts can sometimes merge with yours.
When you are calm, I come to you
And speak in pictures in your mind.
Be attentive to your thoughts and dreams
For in them you'll find me.

We tried to make a heaven of earth,
But the earth is just a stage, a school,
Where we wear our masks and play our roles
And teach each other how to love.

You now ask me where I am.
I'm with you! Where else exists?
There is no "other" place.
There is only one, this one.
I'm not somewhere out beyond the stars!

Do you think that Heaven's far from Earth?
It is not far. They are the same!
The place doesn't change; it's we who do.
The body that you think is "you",
Well, it isn't you at all.
It just contains and separates you
From the Heaven that surrounds.

One day you will leave it too,
Just the way that I left mine.
You'll be surprised but you will find
The moment when you shed your skin,
We'll be together again.
~~~~~~~

It was the first time she hiked the eastern part of the trail since she and I walked it together. She hiked up and up and up to the high places we used to go. She took a breather at the shady little halfway place where we used to stop to rest. She sat down on our big flat rock looking at the view and remembering me there.

My Friend,
Do you see how you cry when you replay
The memories of my week of pain?
Emotional scars take longer to heal,
Shrapnel fragments cut and hurt!
They live on only in your mind.
Don't think of those things any more.

That is not who I was.
That is not who I am.
Don't think of me in pain, I'm not!
Pain and suffering just exist
When you have a body.
Pain is just your messenger,
Telling you it's time for change.
I had to suffer for had I not,

You'd be clinging to me still,
Wanting me to stay with you.

It hurts when someone won't let go.
Not only do we have to leave,
We must tear ourselves from one who clings.
~~~~~~~

Jack...Oh my God. Jack is that you?

She heard me! Oh, She heard me! She spoke to me, her heart to mine!

It is! It is! Yes, it's me! It's me!

Oh Jack, she said, I've missed you so but I've learned I need to let you go. I thought I let you go that night. I didn't realize I've been hanging on. I'm sorry, Jack. I just wanted to do the right thing.

You are. You do. You will. You always do the right thing. You always do the loving thing.

"Is it time for me to scatter your ashes?" she asked me out loud.

Not everyone needs to scatter the ashes but it was right for us.

Yes, scatter the ashes. They are not who I am. They only represent my death. Don't think of me as breathing my last breath. Don't think of how our beautiful life changed overnight. Just think of the gift of our beautiful life.

"You're so right. We had such a beautiful life."

Don't think of Jesus on the cross. This is not how he wants to be remembered either. Set him free from the cross in your mind so he also can rise from your dead. He is not dead! I am not dead! Set us free! By setting us free you set yourself free. Life goes far beyond what you can see or even imagine.

She was crying again, this time because she understood completely that it was time to close this chapter of her grief. She would no longer be death's victim. She knew it was finally time. It was time to let me go.

Suddenly the sound of a great gust of wind approached her from behind. A big cloud of black birds, twenty or more, flew within inches of her head. The group vibration was strong. As she recovered from that, one final bird brought up the rear, skimming the space over her left shoulder. The experience gave her goose bumps much like the ones she sustained when the hummingbird moth visited her on the other side of the trail that day.

Have you noticed that every time you cry something comes and interrupts your tears? That is me. I am unhappy to be the source of your grief. I want you to be happy when you think of me.

"How," she asked, "how do I get over you?"

My Friend....
When you remain attached to me,

You keep the chain around my neck.
Please free me from your leash of love.
By doing so you free yourself.
Remember how I was in life,
Always right beside you?
Always at your feet!
You did not have a leash on me.
There was no fence. I was not chained.
I stayed close by because I loved.

Don't ever question where I've gone or
Where I am when you can't see.
There's nowhere else I am and
There's nowhere else I'd rather be.

~~~~~~~~

She took a deep breath. "I love you Jack. I now know what I have to do."

She resumed walking the trail towards home. The crowd of birds still gathered ahead in the orchard of trees at the curve of the trail. As she rounded the curve, a great view of the western sky opened up. Painted into the setting sun was a cross as straight as could be. It took her breath away. She pulled out her phone and took a picture of it and that picture became the cover of this book.

Three days later, exactly six months to the day after my passing, she took the ashes from off the dresser in the bedroom. She carried them thoughtfully to our special place along the trail where she talked with me. She prayed for me. She prayed for herself. She did not take any of it lightly, nor should she have. It was the biggest Letting Go yet. She would no longer be able to cling to that urn full of ashes.

She took a deep breath and then another. A breath much like when you are standing at the edge of the river and you don't know how cold the water is. Bracing herself. A third breath and she was ready. She threw three handfuls of dust into the air.

I watched her as she set them free with her tears of relief for her and for me. As she scattered them she said to me with a slight smile at the edge of her voice, "I love you enough to let you go. You deserve to be free. Fly Free Little Boy, Fly Free!"

The rest of them she scattered lightly about beneath the trees and at the edge of our path in our special places. Along the way she read Psalm 23 "Ye though I walk through the valley of the shadow," and Ecclesiastes: "Then shall the dust return to the earth as it was, and the spirit shall return unto

God who gave it." She sang the song "Amazing Grace" and thanked God for the gift of me. I was so proud. I was so free...and soon she'd find that so was she.

Not everyone is inspired to spread or bury the ashes. Some will keep them close on their altars or have them poured into crystals or something else, but she did for us what was right for us. She knew I loved our trail and that I would be happy to have them feed the trees we loved so much. They can do more on the trail than they ever could on her dresser in a plastic bag inside a plastic box.

There we were. I was in the corral looking up at her standing high on the hill above me. As she began making her way down to me, I waited at the fence like always, calmly wagging and smiling. As she approached I turned and ran cheerfully to the other side. I'd been waiting for this for such a long time. I had been waiting there for her to open the gate for me.

She was dreaming, but she knew she was, and in her dream she knew what this meant. It was time for me to be free. She wanted me to be happy and she knew she had to open the gate sooner or later. She was the only one who could do it. Now seemed as good a time as any.

She gently took off my collar. I sniffed it for the last time; smelling the lingering traces of my life on earth with her. She opened wide the gate and I ran out into the beautiful field of green grass and yellow flowers, blue skies and sunny day. I ran and ran and ran around, oh I was so happy! I was so free! Then I stopped and looked back at her like I always did; to be sure she was still there or now perhaps to let her know that, no matter what, I still love her best of all.

I romped across the great field to see her one more time before disappearing into the forest. For just a moment I returned to the trees that lined the edge of the meadow for one more glimpse of her. I showed her that I was happy. I told her that I loved her. Then I turned and ran joyfully back into the woods. She waited there until she knew I wouldn't reappear.

Things always come full circle. I waited for her at the puppy mill gate when first we met. I waited until she was ready to free me from that life and become my earthly master. In much the same way I've been waiting again. I've been waiting for her to set me free to be with my Master here.

Upon waking from our dream she cried like she did the night I died. To her I died all over again, but I was reborn too. Finally she'd cut the cord that bound Heaven to Earth and by doing so she set us free.

Now I speak the words to her that she so often said to me:

My Friend...
You stay there. You can't come in.
They don't allow you here.
Everything will be okay.
Wait for me. I'll come back for you.
I promise.

~~~~~~~

And one day, in time that will pass in the blink of an eye, I will meet her at the gate and we will run together through the soft green meadow into a beautiful new world.

My Friend...
Every end is a chance to begin again.
Keep the door of your heart open.
I am always waiting there.
I am always watching, guiding you.
I'll help to untangle the sadness in your heart
And bolster it with hope and faith
That love will come again.

~~~~~~~~~

Where I am now, everyone is the same. We are all lovers. It is only when we come to earth to live out our roles and scripts that we find predators and prey, criminals and victims.

Remember the dream of Hawk you had when I was little? The one who carried me away? How big he was, bigger even than me! He was no ordinary hawk; he was extraordinary. Hawk is an angel! I have met him here and he is teaching me to fly. That's what you saw in your dream. I was learning to fly! That's why I was so proud and happy as I flew along with him! See, it all makes sense now.

Remember Rox the Rottweiler? In his life on earth he seemed so old but here he is young and vibrant and happy, like everyone in Heaven is. This is where we are rewarded, especially if we didn't get back all the love we gave on earth. Love is waiting for us here.

And our friend Lizard, you must remember him. He is here as well. I have learned that lizards are transition specialists. They travel back and forth between the worlds. I don't think you ever knew this, but Lizard first came to us when Grady was leaving. He helped her to find her way to the Rainbow Bridge. Remember when we found him on our fireplace that morning? That's when he came to tell me that he'd be coming back for me. That's why he was there the day you took me to the vet. He knew the plan. He was preparing to help me find my way as well. He wants me to tell you that it's time for you to move on too, into a world of new beginnings.

Oh and by the way, you probably don't want to hear about that little coyote girl, the one who lived around the bend in our road, but she is here and she still likes me! As does the beautiful cream-colored Afghan Hound with her stately nose and long flowing hair who runs over the hills with me. I dreamed of her long before I knew that dreams really do come true.

As for dogs going to Heaven: A dog is always at the door to greet you when you come home, so why would Heaven be any different? Remember how at the dog park the dogs would crowd around the gate when they saw someone approaching? We always know when someone special is arriving here because the dogs run in circles and leap up in the air. They do whatever it is they love to do best, whining in loving welcome to see their friends again. Sometimes their best friends have gotten really old but it doesn't matter because when they come through the gate they are just like the rest of us. The years fade away and they are young again.

My Friend...
Now it's your turn
To learn what you have taught.
It's time for you to Stay. To wait.
Be patient. Sit. Lie down. Relax.

The day will come when you'll be free
From the life that you now know.
When the time is right you'll hear my voice.
You will know it's time to go.
You'll know my voice because it's yours.
"Come! Come Home! C'mon, let's go!"

You'll see me there across the bridge,
Waiting just for you.
You'll know me in a heartbeat,
Your jumping Jacka-KangaRoo!

Just like a dog knows the train will arrive,
I'll know to start looking for you.
We'll, all of us, be here
At the gate to guide you through.
~~~~~~~

She's healing. She doesn't cry so much anymore. It's a lot more fun to visit her now. My friend the Lizard escorts me. My scent still lingers there and every once in awhile she finds another long blonde shiny dog hair. She saves each one.

"Lookie! It's Jackie!" she says with a smile as she purposefully buries each strand in the soil of her houseplants. I watch her for a little while and then Lizard guides me back Home to the Master Over All of Us. Sometimes it's hard to leave her but I know I can always come back.

She learned early in life to believe that love was conditional. My main mission was to teach her that true love has no conditions. That's what most pets come to teach. She was a very good student.

In my 20/20 houndsight it was kind of a divine set up. God sent me to her to teach her how wonderful it is to love and be loved so that when I was gone from her she would yearn for love again. She would no longer be afraid of love. She would learn that love overcomes fear. She would realize that the love we shared was her reward for taking a chance on love, for taking a chance on me.

Some people think they can do it alone but the fact is that while they are on earth, people need each other. They need to be in the company of people who are good for them. When we are well matched we give each other what the other needs. We complete each other and we have a sense of what it's like to be whole and perfect. It's only natural to want to seek completion with another being. Nobody on earth is perfect, although once in awhile they can come close when combined with the right partner. Once we get to Heaven we are each, alone, complete and perfect.

She feels a stirring in her heart. She's starting to look at dogs again. She's a little worried that I'll be jealous, imagining me watching her as if she is replacing me. I am not jealous at all. I don't judge. I trust that she loves me deeply with a love that will not end. I live in a place where jealousy and judgment do not exist; a place that sees the best in everything and I only want what's best for her.

This place I live is incredible. No one is homeless here. We all have beds as soft as clouds and cozy dens made out of love. All dogs are good here because all day long they hear: "Good Dog! Good Dog!"

My Friend...
Open up your beautiful heart.
You think it is broken; shattered?
The heart can never break
If you believe love never dies.
When new love comes to you (it will)
I will not envy because I know
That no one takes my place with you.
I'm in your heart and there I'll stay.
I'll wait without condition

And I will love the ones you come to love.

~~~~~~~

She's looking. She's wondering. She's hoping. She has heard many stories about dogs that returned as little puppies and ended up in the arms of their beloved master again.

She can't help but look for me. She is focusing on young dogs born after the date of my death, just in case one of them might be me, but it is not my personal destiny to return.

Some dogs are fortunate enough to get a master who raises their consciousness to a higher level. Being her dog made me almost human. It raised me and evolved me to the highest dog level possible. Like humans we return only if we have more to learn. If we've learned all of our lessons there's no point in coming back to earth to learn them all again.

One must be careful because in their concerted efforts to find "The Right One", they might find something else instead. They can miss out on the one that was waiting for them while they were looking the other way.

Oh My Friend...
It is wise to be discerning.
There's a dog waiting for you, it's true.
But please don't try to find me.
I am not where you are looking.
Don't agonize about it.

The dog that's meant to be with you
Will simply come at the right time.
You'll find yourself in the right place.
That's how you know it will be yours.
~~~~~~~

She looks at dogs that remind her of me but in her heart she knows that she needs a different kind of dog. She knows she has new lessons to learn from a new teacher.

At the shelters and on YouTube and on Facebook, she cries. The Internet broadcasts and magnifies everything. She sees that there are scams all over the world. They steal photos off legitimate sites, present them as their own dogs, arrange for a deposit and never deliver a dog at all. She has learned the most reputable places to get dogs; rescues and otherwise.

She watches videos and weeps over animals that have been abused, starved, stolen, boxed up, unboxed or cast aside. She becomes immersed in the massive injustices against defenseless animals. The feeling is magnified as one person shares a story and it goes to another and another. The original fear compounds as the news goes viral until all she sees is crime and cruelty in the world. She doesn't really want to look at the raw photos and footage but she cannot help herself. She is only human.

Dogs don't get caught up in this stuff. Yes we live in the moment but at the same time we always remember that there is a life we came from and that life is waiting for us after this one.

Caged animals are not like caged humans. Animals simply accept without complaint whatever happens. All those "urgent" dogs and cats and horses and others waiting to be rescued...they simply tolerate their fate. They know there is more to life than this. They never forget who they are.

John says, "And the light shines in darkness, but the darkness comprehends it not."

Starsky was an Irish Setter who started out sweet and obedient. His family was really mean to him and took him for granted. He soon became a "problem" dog. He acted up and then he acted up some more because what he really wanted was for his owner to surrender him so that he could have a chance at a better life. Animals have a way of knowing certain things and we have a way of making things happen. Starsky's here now and it's wonderful how his name changed to Star Sky. He was destined for this place.

People feel sad because they think their pets don't understand what's going on, but we do. We understand more than you think we do. We accept one who holds dominion over us as long as we are on the earth and we know there is nothing we can do but put our fates in the hands of man. We are always ready to go Home when it's time to go Home. If no one claims us, wants us, or clings to us, it makes it very easy to run right back over that Rainbow Bridge to be with our loving Master in Heaven.

All pets come to this planet to love. Humans come here to love and learn love. While some of them have a harder time with it than others, everybody is doing the best they can.

A person can only love another as much as they love themselves. If a person seems to be unlovable, it is usually because they feel unloved or have never really experienced being loved without condition. The ones that seem to need love the least, well, they usually need it the most...and somebody's got to do it. We are at your service no matter who you are or how you treat us. It's okay because we always know you are doing your best. It's our goal to help you know and recognize what love is. It's our goal to love you with all that we are.

Some people are victims of their own beliefs. They can get stuck in the past and their fear holds them back from living and loving. Animals are different. We live in the possibilities that exist beyond a pessimistic mind that believes the harshness of the world is irreversible. We have faith and we can always see the best in everyone and everything.

When you live in the moment, the past does not exist. It does not matter. When the past does not matter there is nothing to forgive. There is nothing to fear. There is nothing to separate you from unconditional and eternal love.

We forgive and when we do, we no longer see what isn't there. The past is past but it's not like we don't remember. We remember those who hurt us, of course we do. We forget all about it until we are in a moment that reminds us. The hair on our back goes up when we see that person who hurt us. We run from the broom, we cringe from the rolled up newspaper, we avoid the blue and yellow teeter-totter. But we never hold a grudge. We know life is too short to live in fear.

The purpose of life and death is to learn to forgive one another, to live in love instead of fear and to be open to the joys of life that are often blinded by the human shadows of guilt, shame and desire for revenge.

The only cure for fear is perfect love. This is why God created dogs to be partners to man. Dogs pull sleds, guard yards, drive herds and hunt, serve the law, lead the blind and are soldiers in war, but first and foremost they serve as man's best friend. When two or more are bound by love, respect and dedication to working together for a common cause, there is absolutely nothing they can't accomplish together.

No one on earth can do it alone. This is the reason why she and I visited the sick, the dying and the infirmed. There were many of them who were loved, but there were some who had never known love. They were the ones we wanted. We wanted them to know that on this earth they were lovable and we showed them this by loving them. The whole point of life is to learn love. Life is the school, love is the lesson and we are all here to teach each other.

If every homeless pet could be assigned to one lonely human, the world would be a better place. There is enough to go around! Everyone would have at least one good friend in this world before they leave it.

Pets are sent from God for one purpose. That purpose is to love. In our perfect love for you we also honor and obey; worship and adore you. We are God's gift to you and I say that as humbly as a being can say such a thing. You can look into our eyes when we look at you and know that this is true.

We teach you unconditional love until you learn and teach it too. This pure love is God inside. He is in every one of us in the love we have to share. Once you know this kind of love, you will never question love again. You'll know it when you see it. You'll know it when you feel it. You will never be confused by something that is something else.

God sends us to you so that you can learn how much He loves you too. He sees you through our eyes and feels you through our hearts and in this He rejoices. When we love you, He is loving you. By loving us, you love Him too.

My Friend...
God chose me just for you
To show you just how much He loves.
You couldn't see Him but could you see
His love when you saw me?
For I was Him! And you were too!
We saw Him in each other.
That's why I thought we were the same.
Each time my master called I came.
If only you'd respond to Him
The way that I respond to you;
He lets you run but not too far

And if you go too far, you'll pay
The price of going your own way.
Our Master's way is always best,
It's better than our own.
You taught me that and so much more
You taught me: Put my Master first,
So arriving here I already knew
What I was supposed to do.
~~~~~~~

When I died I left my body behind and along with it I left my brain. The brain is part of the body. The brain is not the mind. You bring the mind with you when you come to earth and you take it with you when you go because it belongs to the soul. It belongs to God. Remember the Big Bang? It isn't really yours. It belongs to everyone. It may sound strange but it is true.

I have found the way into her mind. When she sleeps, her overactive brain is sleeping too. The mind takes over, taking her wherever her soul wants to go. Dreams are the meeting places of the soul. Sometimes I can even catch her just before she falls asleep or in the moments when she wakes.

We dreamed a dream again last night. She had driven her car off the road and then she started riding a horse that magically appeared before her. She felt that she loved this horse. They rode slowly out of town into the countryside. Soon they came to a clearing and she got off the horse, but when she turned around it wasn't there. She didn't know how to find it or how to call it to come back. She didn't even know its name. She did all that she knew to do: she whistled the way she had always whistled for me.

In less than a moment there I was, standing at the edge of the forest wagging my tail and waiting for her. The big trees were covered in orange, red and yellow leaves and there was a rainbow carpet of leaves all around. She came to me and we walked along the soft path through the woods to the other side. It was just like old times walking together! At the end of the path she had to keep going and I couldn't go with her. So she went along her way and I went back into the rainbow forest where I thanked my friend the horse for bringing her to me.

When she woke up, she wasn't sad. She was just happy that she had seen me for a little while. All she had to do was whistle.

My Friend, we'll be together again,
And you will know that you are home.
You'll hear me say, "Come Home! Come Home!"
In the meantime, pleasant dreams;
I will see you there.
~~~~~~~~~~

The End

...is just the beginning...

"AfterWords From the Author

I have had dogs in my life since my first year on earth. Each one has been an inspiration and a support. If I am lucky, I will always have dogs.

There are not enough words to capture the magic I have witnessed working with the dying for the past 30 years. This combined with my longtime pursuit of spiritual studies provide the insights and concepts that support Jack in this book. This book may not be for everyone but everyone may have something to learn from it. It is a storybook for all ages filled with the love stories of Jack's life and it is a study guide full of the lessons that we learned together. I was blessed to love and be loved by him.

As Jack says at the very beginning, this is only our story. It reflects our combined beliefs. Just as God is hidden inside of each one of us waiting for us to discover Him when we are ready, God was hidden in this book waiting for you to notice Him. He is not only the Master on these pages but he is 'master' as well. Not only this, but He is Jack, He is you, He is me. Some readers are not ready for Him and this is why we keep His place in the story fairly subtle. Those who know Him will recognize him here. Those who do not know Him, well, I hope you enjoyed our story.

Jack and Kate outside their home in Sedona, Arizona.

If you enjoyed our book, please consider leaving us a review on Amazon so others know it's worth a read! It means so much to us! Thank you!

Other Books in the Jack McAfghan Trilogy:
Book 2: **The Lizard from Rainbow Bridge**
Book 3: **Jack McAfghan: Return from Rainbow Bridge**

We invite you to visit us on Facebook:
Jack: **www.facebook.com/MyJackofHearts**
Our Pet Loss Support Group:
www.facebook.com/groups/edgeoftherainbow
Kate's Website: www.katemcgahan.com
Jack's Blog: www.jackmcafghan.com

Made in the USA
Monee, IL
07 July 2026